2ND EDITION

PLANNING AHEAD

EVERYTHING YOU NEED TO KNOW ABOUT ESTATE PLANNING AND ELDER LAW

MICHAEL MONTEFORTE JR., ESQ.

WORD ASSOCIATION PUBLISHERS
www.wordassociation.com
1.800.827.7903

MONTEFORTE LAW, P.C.
FAMILY • LEGACY • SECURITY

400 Tradecenter, Suite 6890
Woburn, MA 01801

Phone: **978-657-7437**

WWW.MONTEFORTELAW.COM

Printed in the United States of America.

ISBN: 978-1-63385-316-4

Designed and published by

Word Association Publishers
205 Fifth Avenue
Tarentum, Pennsylvania 15084

www.wordassociation.com
1.800.827.7903

DEDICATION

This book is dedicated to the most important people in my life:

To Jill, whose belief in me is astounding, and made my career possible. Sit next to me on the beach forever, my love.

To Gabriella my dancer, and Michael my baseball player, you are why my life has meaning and purpose. Always you.

To Mom, you made me who I am.
You are the strongest person I know.

I love you all.

ATTORNEY MICHAEL MONTEFORTE JR.

First, a little history ...

I GREW UP in Wakefield, MA, and went to Wakefield High from 1990-1994. I then attended Salem State College (now University) where I received the Salem State Presidential Scholarship for academics, and graduated magna cum laude from the Salem State Honors Program in 1998 with a degree in criminal justice. The most important thing that the criminal justice curriculum taught me is that I never wanted to be a criminal lawyer. It was definitely going to be the civil side of the law for me.

I started Suffolk Law School straight out of college, determined to finish in three years, despite having to work nights and weekends. I went to school with other students whose parents paid for their apartments right around the corner from school, while I was either taking the train or fighting the traffic. When I got out of class, I went to one of my two jobs, either the computer store in Woburn or the small law firm in Lynn.

Despite being exhausted most of the time, I graduated from Suffolk after three years, in 2001. I actually took the bar exam and got married all in the same week (bar exam on Wednesday-

Thursday, rehearsal dinner Friday, and wedding Sunday) and still managed to pass on my first try. I was sworn in to the Massachusetts Bar in January 2002.

My wife and I moved to Wilmington in 2003, and we have two children in the Wilmington school system.

I worked as an associate with the Lynn firm until 2006, when I went out on my own, and opened the Law Office of Michael Monteforte Jr. in September 2006. My firm started out as a General Practice, handling pretty much whatever came in the door, but over the years, I started to concentrate on the specific legal fields that I found to be fulfilling and challenging. I began to take continuing education classes that specialized in estate planning and elder law, and honed my expertise in those fields. I was licensed as a New York attorney in 2014.

The firm incorporated in 2017 and underwent a name change, now called Monteforte Law P.C. The firm specializes in estate planning, elder law, and probate/estate matters. We also service clients in real estate and business. For any other areas of law, we can provide referrals, but we are accepting new cases only in those fields.

I am a member of the National Academy of Elder Law Attorneys and part of the Practice Development and Practice Management Section, as well as a member of the Alliances Committee. Several times per year, I attend the Medicare and Elder Law updates put on by the Foundation for Continuing Education, and hold their Certificate in Trust and Estate Planning.

Why do I do this?

It's simple really. My family – starting with my grandparents. Although they are no longer with us, their memory is a constant reminder to me about why I chose this field.

When my firm was still new, my grandparents (to me, Nanny & Papa) decided it would be best to move into an assisted living facility. My grandfather was starting to suffer from dementia, and his symptoms were worsening. It was time for them to live in a setting that offered more specialized care. As we all know, the costs of long-term care are astronomical. During this time, my family and I watched as they drained their savings in order to live comfortably and safely.

My family kept asking me about my grandparents' legal rights, but I was a young lawyer then, and the truth is, I didn't know the answers. I was still perfecting and honing the focus of my practice. I made a pledge to myself then, that I would become educated in the fields of elder law and estate planning. I took this opportunity to read and learn as much as I could to find some way — any way — to help my family. So I read, and I studied, and I attended continuing legal education, so I could learn this field.

Although I was of some help to my grandparents, there wasn't much I could do at that point, because Planning Ahead is the key, and we were already late to the game. But that's when I found my passion. I currently only accept cases in estate planning and elder law. While I have resources and a referral network available for clients needing other forms of legal help, my focus gives me the greatest opportunity to provide as much help as I can.

So that's why I do it, and why I am passionate about it. By helping others, in some small way, it's like I'm helping my grandparents too, and hopefully making them proud. We lost my grandfather in 2017, and my grandmother in 2019. My grandfather left me a ring when he passed away, and I keep it in a display case in my office, where I can see it every day. And it's not just the ring; my office is filled with gifts and decorations they gave me when I was first starting out, and could barely afford to pay the rent. A long time has passed since then, but I can look at these items - the ring, the nameplate on my desk, various trinkets - and feel the joy of when they were still here.

Affiliations

Admitted January 2002, Supreme Judicial Court of Massachusetts

Admitted to federal practice March 2006, US District Court, District of MA

Admitted to US Tax Court

Admitted August 2014, State Supreme Court of New York

Member of National Academy of Elder Law Attorneys (NAELA), Federal and Massachusetts Chapters

Member of NAELA Practice Development and Practice Management Section

Member of NAELA Alliances Committee

Licensed real estate broker

Licensed life insurance producer/broker

Holder of FCLE Certificate in Trust and Estate Planning

Vetted and Approved by Secure Insight for real estate practice

DISCLAIMER

Now that you've got the history, let's start with a disclaimer. Of course, we lawyers always need to start with disclaimers.

Estate planning and elder law is ever-changing. The field is constantly in a state of flux as new laws are enacted, new rules come about, and new cases are decided. Therefore, it is still of paramount importance that you consult with an attorney when considering the information in this publication. Depending on how much time has passed, new rules, laws, and cases may have materialized, all of which would have an effect on the advice and the information that you receive here. This book was written under the current rules and regulations in Massachusetts in 2018. I make no promises as to what changes may occur beyond that time (but if you reach out to us, we can talk about it).

INTRODUCTION

By way of introduction, there are several topics that I intend to cover here. We're going to start with the basics of an estate plan—what it is, what it does, why you need it, and what can happen if you don't have one. Beyond that, we're going to talk a little bit about trusts and how various trusts can play into an estate plan, including the various benefits and potential drawbacks of having a trust. We will discuss different types of trusts and what they can and cannot do. Then we'll get a little bit into the field of elder law. I hate that the field is referred to in that way, as if someone's age is what defines them, but that is the common term of the day. There are some ideas, thoughts, rules and regulations that are important to folks that are getting on in years and there are some special considerations there, whether it's for you or for your parents to be thought about and taken into consideration in your estate plan. Older folks have different needs, and older folks need to think about long-term care, protecting their assets, and who and how they're going to pay for their long-term care. So we'll get into that as well, along with some solutions and potential drafting notes that can assist with those matters.

A NOTE ON SOFTWARE SELF-GENERATED ESTATE PLANS OR "ONLINE" ESTATE PLANS

AN INTRODUCTORY TYPE question that I'm asked a lot is regarding website solutions (you know who they are and you've seen them on TV) and whether or not you really need an attorney to draft your estate plan. In my opinion, it is 100 percent paramount that you have an attorney draft your estate plan. I can't tell you how many times I have reviewed documents prepared by LegalZoom or other canned-type software solutions, where there are tons of errors, tons of incorrect information, and very often, incorrect references to the law.

For example, I reviewed documents that were supposed to be for clients in Massachusetts and those documents contained references to California law!! And the client had no idea!! Once I reviewed their documents and pointed out these errors, we had to scrap the old documents and start from scratch. So that client went and spent a couple of hundred dollars for cheap estate documents, then came to me later on for a review. All of the documents they had paid for were no good, so they essentially wasted a couple of hundred dollars. I had to tear everything up and do everything fresh. I had hoped to salvage some of those documents for the client and save him some money, but they were ripe with errors, inconsistencies, and bad information.

That's not to say that these software solutions are never the appropriate answer. For example, they are appropriate if you don't have a lot of assets. The reference number I like to use is $25,000, because in Massachusetts, anyone with under $25,000 in assets can file a simplified probate. So if you've got under $25,000, and you don't have money to spend on an estate lawyer, something is better than nothing. Having any Will is better than having no Will.

Therefore, if all you can afford is a couple of hundred dollars, and you have to use a website solution, or an automated solution, something is better than nothing. But it should definitely be a temporary answer, not a permanent one. The goal should be to later have an estate plan attorney review those documents that you receive, and try to salvage what they can while drafting you a good plan. But in my experience, those software-generated documents just aren't very good.

To do it right, you need to have your situation evaluated. You need to have an attorney who looks at these things on a case-by-case basis. I draft custom solutions for each client and for that client's particular situation. I do an interview with the client, I think about their information, I sit down and digest everything that's in my file and in my notes, and I use that to come up with a custom recommended solution for that client. I tailor my documents to that particular client's needs. The reality is that you get what you pay for in estate planning—custom documents are the key, even though it costs more.

It's not about upselling. I don't give my clients any documents that they don't need. I don't sell them anything beyond what their situation calls for. But, using a computerized or internet solution simply doesn't have the capacity to look at all the factors and provide what's best.

PART I

ESTATE PLANNING

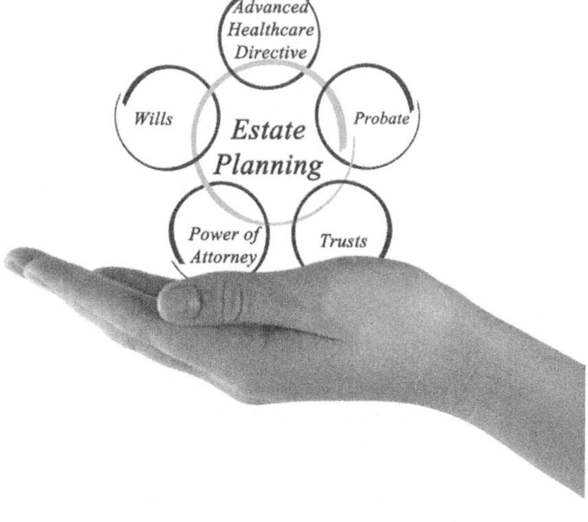

CHAPTER 1

WHAT IS AN ESTATE PLAN?

So what is an estate plan? Lots of people ask me "Do you do Wills?" Well, at my firm we don't just draft "Wills," we draft estate plans. Wills are an integral part of that plan. Think of it like a jigsaw puzzle, where each document is an individual puzzle piece. The pieces have to work together to make the picture, and that picture is the estate plan.

An estate plan can consist of a myriad of documents, ranging from Wills and trusts to more sophisticated estate planning tools, depending on the situation, the client, and what that client's particular family orientation and assets call for. The very basics in an estate plan come down to what I like to call The Big Three. An estate plan is not complete without these three essential documents. The first document is, as I'm sure you'd guess, a last Will and testament, or just commonly referred to as a Will. Almost everyone has heard of the Will, knows what a Will is, and what it does. We will get into that further, discussing what's required to be in a Will, what is common, what's not common, and special considerations that need to be taken. So that's number one of The Big Three—the Will.

Number two of The Big Three is the power of attorney, or POA. And lastly, number three of The Big Three is the health care proxy.

In my opinion, for an estate plan to even be called an estate plan here in Massachusetts, you've got to have those three documents. Everyone knows what a Will does—it directs where you want your property to go when you pass away. The power of attorney allows you to name somebody that can make financial decisions for you in the event that you can't make them for yourself and in certain situations sign your name for you. The health care proxy allows you to name someone to make health care decisions for you in the event that you can't do so for yourself.

Those three documents are crucial to any estate plan. There are other documents that can be just as important. For example, certain types of trusts, which will be discussed later. And there are other ancillary documents that allow you to express things like burial wishes and so forth. But the Will, the health care proxy, and the power of attorney are the most important and the foundation of any estate plan. Other documents can be added or taken away later. But you need those three to even call it a "plan."

CHAPTER TWO

WHAT IF I DON'T HAVE A WILL?

BEFORE WE GET into a substantial discussion of The Big Three documents and any other documents, let's talk a little bit about what happens if you don't have a Will. While I am referring here to Massachusetts law, be mindful that every state has its own laws if someone passes away and there is no last Will and testament. Those laws are called intestacy laws, and you can be said to have died "intestate" if you have no Will.

There are lots of misconceptions about what happens if you die without a Will. And those rules changed a few years back in Massachusetts when we enacted what's called the Massachusetts Uniform Probate Code or MUPC, which is codified in M.G.L. c. 190B. The uniform probate code really turned the old intestacy laws upside down and changed things.

In my experience, many people think if they pass away, their spouse is automatically going to get everything, so they don't need a Will. Well, in Massachusetts, that's not necessarily true. If you have a spouse and children, or either spouse has children from another relationship, and you pass away without a Will, i.e., intestate, everything does <u>not</u> go directly to your spouse.

Instead, there's a division between your spouse and your kids. People use this erroneous way of thinking as an excuse as to why they don't need an estate plan—"my spouse gets it all, so I don't need one." I hear it all the time. Although you may be thinking that your spouse is going to get everything, the MUPC says otherwise. That's because if you pass away intestate, your kids, and even sometimes your parents, have certain rights, and both biological children and adopted children are treated the same way (as they should be). Under the MUPC, if you die intestate, and have both a spouse and children, but either spouse has children from outside that marriage, then your spouse inherits, along with the children, according to a chart set forth in M.G.L. c. 190, Section 2-102 (see below). Therefore, there can be situations where funds that you thought were going to your spouse don't end up there.

Without a Will in place, you could be leaving your spouse in trouble and impoverished. This has happened to several clients of mine, where a surviving spouse came to me to probate an intestate estate, only to find out that they would be sharing what they thought was theirs alone. In many such situations, the children will disclaim, or waive, their rights to the inheritance so that the surviving spouse can inherit the estate. But that's not always the case. People do strange things when there is money involved, especially desperate people, and children can assert their rights under the intestacy laws and claim their piece, even if it leaves Mom or Dad in a bad way. I've seen it happen, and nothing can be done about it. I even had a surviving wife who had to sell her home because she needed the money, after her husband's child asserted her intestacy rights! If that's not enough to convince you that you need a Will, I'm not sure what is.

Although this is not the place for a detailed discussion about various intestacy situations, here are some common intestate scenarios under the MUPC:

If the surviving spouse has any living children from another marriage or relationship in addition to living children of the marriage to the decedent, the surviving spouse now takes the first $100,000 of the probate estate, plus one half (½) of the balance. The decedent's children take the rest.

If there are surviving children of the decedent from another marriage or relationship, the surviving spouse now takes the first $100,000 of the probate estate, and one half (½) of the balance of the estate, if any. The decedent's children from all marriages or relationships take the rest.

If the decedent has no descendants, but is survived by a parent or parents, the surviving spouse takes the first $200,000 of probate property, and takes three-quarters (¾) of the balance of the probate estate (an increase from one half of the balance under former law). The surviving parent(s) will take the rest.

Another reason why it's important to have a Will, and potential resulting negative effects of not having one, have to do with the probate process. The probate process, if there's no Will, can be much longer, it can be much more expensive, and there can be a lot more involved when it comes to probate filing. You're going to be spending a lot more money on attorney's fees, and a lot more time dealing with the court. A Will helps you avoid this because a Will sets out what's going to happen and doesn't leave any guesswork for the court or your beneficiaries to deal with, and thus doesn't leave your family stuck with having to go by the intestacy laws that may or may not do what you want. As we saw, those laws may or may not leave your assets in the manner that you wanted them to be left.

CHAPTER 3

WHAT DOES A WILL COVER?

Another common question that I get a lot is people asking what's covered by a Will. "Does everything come under my Will?" The answer is no. A Will only deals with what are called probate assets, and probate assets are assets that are in the deceased person's name alone at the time they pass. So if you own assets jointly with somebody else, with rights of survivorship, and you pass away, those assets become the property of the joint owner solely. If you've got a joint bank account with rights of survivorship and you pass away, the person that you are jointly on the account with now owns those assets and those assets don't have to go through probate. They are not covered under your Will, because they were jointly owned; they are not probate assets.

Now why is that important? Number one, it has to do with speed. Beneficiaries of those assets can obtain those assets right away; they don't have to wait for the court to say it's OK. Another factor has to do with creditors. If you have creditors and they come in and try and file claims against your estate, those creditors are limited to your estate assets or probate assets. Creditors can't reach to property that's not included in probate. So, things like joint assets, which pass automatically to the surviving owner, all avoid probate. They can't be attached by creditors in most circumstances. And, they're going to be disbursed to beneficiaries right away.

Another example of what can be non-probate assets is life insurance. If you have life insurance and you have named life insurance beneficiaries, those beneficiaries will receive the proceeds of your life insurance directly, and probate is not involved. The assets skip over probate and go directly to the beneficiary. No probate is needed.

Lastly, retirement accounts can be non-probate assets. Many of those accounts give you an opportunity to name beneficiaries. And in those cases, if you name beneficiaries and those beneficiaries survive you, those assets can avoid probate.

I always tell my clients to try and keep as many assets out of probate as possible for those reasons. And I counsel them on that during the estate planning process, so that the Will is only left dealing with assets that couldn't otherwise be given directly to beneficiaries or owned jointly with joint owners. There are exceptions when your beneficiaries are minors, when they are too young to obtain substantial assets or any assets, depending on their age. And those assets can be controlled by their guardians. In those cases, we may want probate to be involved, to oversee things.

For the above reasons, I ALWAYS encourage my clients to keep their beneficiary info up to date. What happens to those accounts if there are no beneficiaries, or if the beneficiaries die before you? As you can probably guess, if there are no living beneficiaries, the funds revert to the estate. They are now probate assets, coming under the Will, and they are subject to estate creditors.

I have many clients that will update their beneficiary info when we are doing their estate plan, but they neglect to keep up with it. One in particular named only his spouse, and she predeceased him. So when he passed, the funds became probate assets, instead of passing directly to his children, and his estate creditors took a big bite out of the funds before the kids finally got their shares. Beneficiary designations should be reviewed at least annually and updated as needed.

CHAPTER 4

THE LAST WILL AND TESTAMENT

So now, let's talk about the last Will and testament, as it is the cornerstone of the estate plan. The person who creates a Will is called the testator or testatrix (silly names, I know).

First of all, what's required for a valid Will in Massachusetts? Some people think they can write something down on a napkin and sign it and it becomes a valid Will. Well, every state has its own rules. A Will that's handwritten or written on a napkin is called a "holographic" Will. Some states recognize holographic Wills and some do not. Massachusetts does not recognize holographic Wills, if they are missing certain key components. Massachusetts law requires that your Will be witnessed by two disinterested parties and that the Will has to be notarized. Also, the testate, or the person writing the Will, has to be over the age of eighteen, of sound mind, and free from coercion or undue influence. Those are the legal, minimum requirements to have a valid Will. Now, when we draft a Will for a client, we put a lot more than that. There's a big difference between a document that just barely meets the legal requirements versus a good document. We draft a document that deals with many different potential situations, so that there's nothing left to chance.

The Will is required to have a notary stamp and have two witnesses. If those requirements are met, whether the Will is written on paper or written on napkin (don't ask me how you would get a notarization on a napkin), my opinion is that the Will can be recognized. When we draft a Will, we're trying, to some extent, to predict the future. We are attempting to contemplate numerous situations that could come to pass and reflect the testator's wishes in all potential scenarios.

Everyone is basically familiar with the point of a Will. It's supposed to indicate where your property is going and where you want your stuff to go when you pass away. And Wills can be very, very specific or they can be very, very general. I've got clients that come in and tell me they want to leave everything to their kids. Throw everything in the pot and leave it all to the children in equal shares. But sometimes I get people that have very, very specific wants when it comes to distribution of their assets. They've come with extensive lists of specific assets and who they want to receive each of those assets.

Most commonly, we hear clients' wishes somewhere in the middle. We get folks that say, "Well, give everything in equal shares to my beneficiaries, but I have one, two, three pieces of personal property that I want to specifically designate." Just for an example from my own estate plan, everything is left to my wife. But, if my wife predeceases me, then everything is left equally to my kids. However, there are provisions in there that say my daughter receives my wife's jewelry and my son receives my watches. I have some fancy watches that my son likes; he's had his eye on them (if I suddenly "fall" off a cruise ship, and you then see my son wearing a Rolex, be suspicious!). So, my

Will says that he is to receive those watches. And it's important that those provisions are in the Will because, right now, my children are young and if a personal representative were to take over and not know that I wanted my kids to have those items, they could sell those items and add the money into the estate pot, rather than give the kids those pieces of personal property like I wanted. Without those provisions, the personal rep. can sell them and turn them into cash assets for the estate, and that's not what I want. I wanted to make sure my son gets these watches and my daughter gets my wife's jewelry. The Will allows us to state that.

Your Will has to name a personal representative. That's the updated term for the old term "executor" that everyone used before the MUPC. Massachusetts changed the terminology back in 2012 with the MUPC. We don't use the term "executor" anymore. The term that we use in Massachusetts is called "personal representative," and that name took the place of the old term, "executor." While we tell clients that in Massachusetts you have to name your personal representative, it's also a good idea to name someone else as a contingency. You can name one person and then a back-up person to take over if the original person that you named is unable to serve. The personal representative has a "fiduciary duty" to your estate and to your beneficiaries. That means the personal representative has a legal obligation to act in the best interest of the beneficiaries.

The job of the personal representative is to take your Will and to present it to the probate court. They can do that with an attorney or they can do it on their own. It's usually much faster if you have an attorney who knows what documents need to be drafted and the attorney submits those documents to the probate court.

Then what has to happen is the court reviews the Will and can make an official appointment of that person to be named the personal representative of the estate. Bear in mind, there are certain other emergency measures that can be taken if for some reason a personal representative needs to be appointed right away, for example if assets are going to be lost or destroyed. The court does have short-term, temporary appointments to deal with any emergency situations. But barring that, the personal representative files with the probate court to be appointed and the probate court can then appoint that person as a personal representative. There are opportunities for beneficiaries to offer their consent, or to object. But when there's a Will, the named personal representative has the priority when it comes to the right to be appointed.

The named individual in the Will has a priority. It doesn't matter whether you're married, not married, have kids, or don't have kids. The person that you name in your Will has priority to be your personal representative. If you don't have a Will, then there is a priority list that the state provides, starting with your spouse and then moving on to your adult children.

Many clients of mine want their children to be their beneficiaries but in no way want them to be the personal representative. So again, it's very important that your Will designate who you want your personal representative to be, with some contingency names as well.

The death of a loved one is obviously an emotional and traumatic experience. It can be overwhelming, especially for the person who is appointed as the personal rep. of the estate. Our website has a checklist that can be downloaded for free, and used by a personal rep. that contains the important steps they should take.

We look at a Will like a set of instructions. You set out a list of instructions for your personal representative and your personal representative is bound to follow those instructions. You're telling your personal representative what assets you want to go where and when your personal representative is appointed, their appointment gives them authority to collect your assets, and to deal with banking institutions, retirement companies, and other types of financial institutions so that they can gather those assets. They then have to report to the court what assets they've gathered. And that's called an Inventory. Then they have to take that inventory and apply the rules that you've set forth in your Will. The personal representative disburses those assets to the beneficiaries that you've named in your Will and the personal representative is bound to show the beneficiaries and the court that they did as they were instructed, via the filing of an "Account."

Remember, a Will can disburse everything from cash assets, bank accounts assets, real estate, real property, and personal property. This includes cups, plates, dishes, jewelry, watches, and those sorts of things. Another important piece that we include on our Wills is the authority for your personal representative to deal with real estate. Here in Massachusetts, if your Will does not specifically give your personal representative the right to deal with real estate, then your personal representative has to apply separately to the court for that authority (that's what we call in Massachusetts a petition for "license to sell"). So even though the Will may dictate where certain property needs to go, if there is no authority to deal with real estate, the personal representative has to file a separate petition with the court, aside from the standard probate of the Will. This extra process, the petition for a license to sell, can be lengthy and expensive. They've got to pay attorneys' fees for an attorney to file it.

We make sure that all of our Wills include and specifically detail the personal representative's authority when it comes to real estate. Your Will should say, "Hey, my personal representative has the right to deal with any real estate that I own, whether it's keeping it, selling it, renting it, mortgaging it, whatever." As long as you say, "My personal rep. has the authority to deal with that," then no license to sell is needed. But, if that is absent from the Will, no matter what your intentions were, your personal rep. has to go through that separate license to sell process. And I can't tell you how many times we've represented clients where we've had to do the license to sell process because the Will was silent on this issue or was not specific enough.

That reference to real estate and the personal rep.'s authority has to be specific, it has to be explicit, and there has to be no question that you intended to impart this authority on your personal rep. to deal with your real estate. And if it's not explicit, then it doesn't exist, as far as the court is concerned. Without it, the license to sell process has to be started in order to sell the deceased person's home. That process takes time and there are sales that are lost because buyers may not want to wait for the license to sell process to be completed.

I've had clients where several buyers have walked away because they didn't want to wait for the additional time needed for the license to sell. When the court is involved in this License to Sell, it's impossible to come up with a set closing date, because the court does things in its own time. It can take weeks, or it can take months, depending on docket congestion. We even had a situation where the court LOST our original petition; they could only find a copy, and the judge refused to grant our petition until the original was found by the clerks—it took MONTHS! The entire license to sell mess is a process that you can spare your beneficiaries of, as long as your Will details the authority for real estate. Ours always do.

Another item to consider when having your Will drafted is guardianship of your minor children. Your Will is the place to nominate guardians for your kids in the event that both parents pass away. This takes special consideration, not just about the guardian themself, but also the location where the guardian lives, whether the guardian has other children, and the guardian's financial situation. All of these factors must be considered when naming a guardian.

Here is a brief note about Will contests. Sometimes, a family member or beneficiary will try to challenge the validity of the Will. As we know, your Will has to be signed, it's got to be notarized, and it's got to be witnessed. You have to be of sound mind in order to create your Will, and free from undue influence or coercion. A Will can be challenged for failure to comply with the rules for the document itself (no notary, no witness) but even more common are challenges to the decedent's ability to make the Will, especially if that decedent was of advanced age at the time of drafting. One of the reasons where beneficiaries can potentially challenge a Will is to say that the testator was not of sound mind when they drafted it and signed it. Another reason for Will challenge could be to state that the testator was under somebody's undo influence or coercion, arguing that when they created their Will, they were influenced by somebody to draft the Will in a certain way that they otherwise would not have. Those are basic reasons that a Will can be challenged. We are especially careful when we have clients come in to sign their documents that we follow all the appropriate measures. We often speak to our clients alone, away from their children, to make sure there is no undue influence happening. We do all we can to make it very, very difficult for somebody to challenge a Will.

Clients sometimes ask about disinheriting a child. Often it's because they've taken care of that child during their lifetime, so they want to leave their estate to their other children. A common practice used to be leaving that child one dollar as a way of showing that you didn't forget that child and that what you wanted to do was intentional. It's no longer necessary to leave the child a dollar; we simply put a provision in our Will that says, "Any kids that I didn't name here, I did that on purpose. It was my intentional act not to name anybody else." We can get more specific if the client requests, and sometimes I have clients that want to explicitly state their reason for leaving a child out. And again, most of the time it's because they may have given assets to that child during their lifetime. If the client prefers, we can put that in the document as well, for clarification.

Along with the details about how you want your personal representative to handle your intangible property, like bank accounts, we also include with our Wills an attachment dealing with personal property—your "stuff." You can attach to your Will a list of personal property that you want to leave to certain individuals and designate who you want to leave that property to. That is accomplished with a memo or a list that you attach to your Will. The reason we do it as an attachment is because that list is not subject to the same notarization and witnessing standards as your original Will. In other words, you can tear that list off any time you want and replace it without having to go through the same formalities as your initial Will signing.

Then, if you later dispose of some of the property on your list or you gave it to the person while you're still alive, you can simply tear up that list and start again. Those are just some of the important parts that go into the Wills that we draft. There's a lot more to it, and a lot of other provisions that we make part of our Wills.

It's almost universal that Wills that were drafted prior to the enacting of the MUPC are relatively short, between three and five pages. They're about double that now because the uniform probate code requires us to list additional information and statutory provisions that were not required in the past. People come to me and ask me to review Wills that were made ten to fifteen years ago and they're so short and they ask why the new documents are so long. It is because of the uniform probate code. In order to draft the documents correctly under those rules, the documents are a bit lengthier. If you have a Will that is pre-2012, you should have it reviewed by an experienced estate planning attorney. Most of the Wills I see from that time period are in need of updates.

CHAPTER 5

THE POWER OF ATTORNEY

NUMBER TWO OF The Big Three (as you now know, the Will is number one) is the durable power of attorney, or POA. The power of attorney is where you designate someone (or someones) to make financial decisions for you, sign documents for you, or do anything financially that you can't do yourself. Your attorney in fact is authorized to perform certain acts on your behalf, and manage your affairs. You may give as much or as little power to your attorney in fact as you see fit. This is another document that I am asked to review very frequently. People will bring me these one- or two-page power of attorney documents that are just terrible because they don't have enough information for your designated person (called your attorney in fact) to deal with various situations. Know that the phrases are commonly interchangeable, calling someone your power of attorney or your attorney in fact, as both mean the same thing.

There is a difference between a power of attorney and a durable power of attorney, or DPOA. The "durable" part is used when the POA is not affected by your subsequent incapacity, and to be durable, it must be specifically stated as such. That's what the durable part means, and we use it for most of our clients. In most cases, we want the authority to continue if the principal (the maker of the POA) were to lose their competency or be medically unable to handle their affairs. A DPOA can be hugely important when trying to move assets for a spouse that is seeking Medicaid/MassHealth benefits; however, your DPOA must specifically allow for such transfers (which is again why we don't like fill-in or canned documents—they usually miss this part).

If you execute a durable POA, and name someone to be your attorney in fact, we always recommend that you also name an individual or individuals to be your backup or successor attorney in fact. You can name one person, or you can name two or more to perform jointly, and it's good to always have some backup individuals named in case that first person cannot serve as your power of attorney for some reason. The power of attorney is very flexible; there are lots of different options. Most clients sign the power of attorney and make it effective immediately when it comes to their spouse. They're giving immediate authority for their spouse to sign for them whenever it is convenient. But then, as to the backup person, whether it be their children or somebody else, we don't often want to make that power immediate unless there's some real need for it. Instead, we make that backup person's power what's called a "springing power."

A springing power is a power that arises later, after the time of document signing. With a springing power, the backup power of attorney doesn't have any authority to act on the principal's behalf unless and until that person becomes incapacitated. And to take it a step further, our documents specify that the principal's incapacity has to be proven via a letter or report from your doctor and be attached to the written POA, attesting to your condition and diminished capacity. Your backup power of attorney can be given their authority right away if the situation warrants it. But most of the time, the POA is the client's child, and we often don't want our kids to have that type of access while we're still kicking, or while we still have our wits about us.

Aside from the springing power, there are lots of other options for the POA. For example, power of attorney documents can be very general; I don't like those kind. I like the document to be very specific and contemplate numerous possibilities. My documents list out as many potential situations as possible, so that there's never any question that the attorney in fact is acting within their authority and no question as to what they are authorized to do. You don't want to have your power of attorney go to a bank and have a bank employee look at the document and say, "Well, I don't really see that the proper authority is granted here. This power of attorney is too general; I can't give you any account access." We make our documents specifically indicate or dictate what type of authority is granted and when it can be exercised, so that financial institutions have no doubt.

Just recently, I had a client with an existing POA document, and we did a Medicaid application for her. We got the application approved, but as part of the approval, assets had to be taken out of the applicant's name. She had an investment account with a brokerage firm, and that firm refused to accept the POA as written, stating that it did not provide the attorney in fact with clear authority. This could have been disastrous, because without the POA, it would have taken a probate petition and court order to move the assets, and MassHealth was only giving us ninety days to make the transfer. Luckily, this client was still competent enough that I was able to draft a new POA and she could sign it. My document, drafted the right way, satisfied the brokerage firm and we were able to transfer the funds, which

(1) saved the MassHealth approval and (2) kept the client from having to shell out more money to the nursing home.

Another part of a power of attorney that has to be very specific has to do with gifts and what's called "self-dealing." Self-dealing is when the power of attorney transfers the assets of the principal to themself, which of course can seem suspect. An attorney in fact is bound to act in the best interest of the principal, so it could appear odd, and even nefarious, for the attorney in fact to transfer the principal's assets to himself or herself, and it naturally invites much scrutiny of the document itself. But bear in mind that much of the time, the attorney in fact is the spouse of the principal. There are very specific times and reasons when it can be necessary for the attorney in fact to make those kinds of transfers. For example, if we have a situation where a husband and wife are each other's POA, and one of them may be going into a nursing home and trying to apply for long-term care benefits, it may be entirely necessary for the healthy spouse to transfer assets out of the name of the spouse who is entering the nursing home. Long-term care coverage underMassHealth is an asset-based benefit, andin circumstances where the nursing home resident has too many assets, it could become necessary to move the assets out of the nursing home resident's name, so that he/she will qualify for those benefits. Therefore, what the healthy spouse will do is transfer assets out of their spouse's name and put the assets into their own name. Such an action, even between spouses, is still self-dealing, and will be scrutinized by both the benefit provider and the various financial institutions.

To allow these transfers, the document has to specifically state the authority granted, or those types of transfers can be voided or access to the account denied. We want spouses or even the other power of attorney to be able to transfer assets so that the principal can qualify for benefits. We don't want them stuck owning assets that disqualify them for benefits. Remember, you need to have great trust in the individuals that you name as your power of attorney for this very reason, as you don't want to name anybody that you'd be afraid could take the assets and put them toward their own use. The entire purpose of power of attorney is to act in the best interest of the principal. But, there has to be specific authority for them to be able to transfer assets to themself or somebody else. And again, the reason for that is being able to qualify for long-term care benefits.

Another POA option is specific authority for the power of attorney to continue operating an ongoing business that the principal was running. If you've got a principal that runs a business and then becomes incapacitated, there has to be specific authority in the POA for their power of attorney to run that business. Otherwise, other employees or anybody could dispute it and say that there is no right in the power of attorney to run the business on behalf of the principal. This can lead to lawsuits, and potentially the need for a petition and court order to deal with the principal's business. We specifically include those types of provisions in our documents so that there's never any question about what the principal intended the power of attorney to be able to do. That way, the attorney in fact doesn't have any problem performing his or her duties, and doesn't have to deal with potential denials from financial institutions.

We want everything to be crystal clear on what you intended your attorney in fact to do. In recent times, power of attorney documents have come under fire for not giving someone the specific authority to deal with nursing homes or long-term care facilities. Very often, someone going into long-term care or a nursing home doesn't have the legal capacity to sign the documents required for entry to the nursing home. Those are legal documents that need to be signed and someone that doesn't have sufficient capacity can't sign them. However, if the document is drafted correctly, we look to the attorney in fact to sign those documents and the power of attorney document has to specifically state that the attorney in fact has authority to deal with nursing homes and long-term care. If not, nursing home and long-term care facilities can refuse to allow the attorney in fact because that authority is not specifically stated, which can result in the need for—you guessed it—a probate petition and court order. Once again, this can be time-consuming and expensive. We make sure our POAs include provisions for that.

I want to share a story with you about a past client that had no power of attorney in place. The client was a single mom who lived in her home with her young child. She was not married, and all of her assets were solely in her name. This client was unfortunately involved in an auto accident, and fell into a coma. The client's mom came to see us about what to do with the daughter's bills that were not being paid, including mortgage and utilities, during the daughter's incapacity. Let me tell you that this story has a happy ending. She eventually came out of the coma and she was fine, no worse for the wear, and healthy, with no additional problems. But during the time that she was in a coma, the individual had no power of attorney document created, so she hadn't designated anybody to make financial decisions or sign documents for her.

This client owned a home. She had a job. She had money in the bank. The problem was, there was no way for our client's mom, or anyone else, to access any of those funds. There was no way for the mom to pay for her daughter's care while she was in a coma. There was no way to pay the daughter's mortgage, no way to pay credit card bills, and no way to pay the daughter's utilities. Meanwhile, there was plenty of money in the bank to cover these expenses, but no way to access it! Mom couldn't afford to pay these bills on her own, and so the creditors had begun to swoop in, demanding their money and making reports to the credit bureaus.

Because there was no power of attorney in place, Mom came to see me, telling me, "My daughter's in a coma. The mortgaging bank is threatening to foreclose on her house, the gas company's going to shut the gas off, and the electric company's going to shut the lights off because I can't pay them. I don't have the money to pay them myself. My daughter has the money. She has a good job. She has money in the bank. In fact, she's received paychecks since the time that she's been in a coma. But no one has authority to sign the checks or deposit the checks, and even if we could, we can't get the money back out because we've got no access to her bank accounts. Nobody at the mortgaging bank will talk to us because we're not authorized on the account. We don't have authority to speak to anybody. We don't have authority to pay any of these bills. My daughter has money in the bank and her house is going to get foreclosed on while she's in a coma."

In that situation, our plan was to file with the court for either a guardianship or a conservatorship, or both, for the client. A guardianship petition asks the court for authority over the person, over the person's body, over their health care, and what happens to them personally. A conservatorship petition asks the court for authority over someone's money and property. What we were going to have to do was petition the court to have Mom appointed as a guardian and conservator. It's a probate petition, again, that can be expensive and lengthy, and requires evidence from the person's doctor clearly stating that the person is incapacitated, is in a coma, or is in some sort of state where they can't take care of themselves. It's a very big deal to go to the court and ask the court to grant someone authority over another person's money. These types of petitions are heavily scrutinized, and again, they can be lengthy and costly.

What we ended up doing was preparing all the documentation, getting ready to go to court, and then, by a miracle, the daughter woke up. She was fine. We didn't have to go through with the petition to get Mom appointed because once the daughter was awake, she could sign documents and sign checks and pay her bills. The story had a happy ending, but if the coma had lasted much longer, the financial picture could have been much worse, not to mention the damage done to the client's credit.

However, that situation could have been completely avoided if the daughter had executed a health care proxy and a power of attorney (and you bet she did them after!). The power of attorney would have let Mom go to the bank with the power of attorney document, and provide a letter from the doctor attached to that power of attorney stating that the daughter was incapacitated. Mom could then access the daughter's bank accounts for the benefit of the daughter, act in the best interest of the daughter, pay the mortgage, pay the bills, pay the utilities, pay the life insurance bill, pay the medical bills, and pay for child care. And all without having to go to the court, and without having to spend the time and the money to do a probate petition. Just having this one document would have saved Mom thousands of dollars in legal fees and mortgage interest, because mortgage interest accrues every single day, with late charges and credit reporting. If the daughter had had a power of attorney, Mom could've marched right down to the bank, gotten access immediately, and paid those bills.

One other document that goes along with the POA is the burial directive. You can state your wishes as far as burial versus cremation, preference for a religious ceremony, or not, and any other specifics you might want for services.

CHAPTER 6

THE HEALTH CARE PROXY

THE THIRD DOCUMENT in that "Big Three" of estate planning is called the health care proxy. There are some ancillary documents that go hand in hand with the health care proxy, but let's start with the health care proxy itself. What is it?

A health care proxy is a document where you designate an individual to make decisions concerning your health care. This is not something used to take away your own decision-making power. As long as you are competent, only you are in charge of these decisions, but if you become incapacitated or don't have your mental faculties, the proxy acts on your behalf. The proxy document can include several options, and should include special revisions regarding nursing home admittance and care.

The biggest fear when it comes to executing a health care proxy is the thought of losing control over one's own decision-making. We are careful to stress to the client that the person they appoint cannot make decisions that go against what you want. As long as you are able to express yourself, there's no need (and no legal authority) for a health care proxy to act for you. But if you lose the ability to express yourself, you're in a coma, or you're in the midst of a surgery, your medical providers can turn to your health care proxy and that health care proxy can make decisions on your behalf. Again, it is only in the event that you can't do so for yourself.

Many clients appoint a spouse and, like all the other documents we've discussed, we find that it's a good idea to appoint at least one backup person, just in case the original proxy could not be available or could not be reached.

The primary worry for clients, as stated, is about control—having control over their own lives and their own medical procedures. We make it clear to our clients, as part of their consultation, that the health care proxy doesn't change that. The health care proxy comes into play in an emergency situation or if you cannot make your wishes known. The other thing that the health care proxy does is it keeps other family members from (1) having to argue about what procedures you may want or not want, and (2) having to argue about who will make decisions on your behalf. You have designated a person or persons to act as a health care proxy for you and that person has your express authority to act on your behalf; therefore, you don't have other family members attempting to make decisions with your doctors or otherwise be involved with the decision-making because you've nominated these individuals already. The health care proxy doesn't leave it up to chance as far as which of your relatives, friends, or family members may attempt to speak on your behalf. It eliminates any gray area because you've clearly named someone to act for you.

The health care proxy is a flexible document that can contain limitations on the authority that you want to give to your health care proxy. For example, I've had clients that have objected to certain types of medical procedures due to religious reasons.

Some religions don't allow blood transfusions, so a person naming a health care proxy to act for them wants to put that limitation in the document, to say that, "My health care proxy can make decisions for me, but at no time should I be given a blood transfusion because it's against my religious beliefs." That's just one sort of limitation that you could put on a health care proxy. Another example would be limiting the type of care you want to receive in the event that you were to suffer from dementia later in life. In that case, you can limit things like forced feeding and medications. There are additional documents that can be drafted and signed, along with the health care proxy which might make additional qualifications to the document itself.

There are documents that I mentioned that go along with the health care proxy. One of those is called a "Living Will." It's a strange name because the document is not actually a Will at all, and people get confused because of the name and think that it's similar to a last Will and testament. It is not. So what is a living Will? It's basically a document that sets out certain parameters for which you would not want to be kept alive if you were in a vegetative, brain-dead state, and gives your proxy and your doctors permission to "pull the plug," rather than keep your body alive while your brain is essentially dead. For example, if you are in a permanently vegetative state, and your medical providers agree that you are not going to wake up, that you don't have any brain activity, but that respiration and feeding tubes could keep you alive for an indefinite amount of time, the living Will allows you to express the fact that you don't wish to be kept alive in that manner.

Let me be clear in saying that a living Will is not a legally binding document in Massachusetts. If the living Will isn't legally binding, then why have one? It doesn't carry legally binding weight, but what it does is it allows an individual, called the principal, to express his or her wishes when it comes to being kept alive on machinery such as respirators and feeding tubes. The living Will is used to express your wishes to your health care proxy, your medical providers, and your family. Even though it's not legally binding, it provides evidence that can be taken into consideration later, if you aren't able to make your own decisions.

The living Will is not for everybody. It's a matter of personal choice for the client, but it is becoming more and more common. And even though it does not have a legal significance, it does two things. First, it acknowledges that you have named a health care proxy to make decisions for you; however, this particular decision of not wanting to be kept alive on these types of machines was a decision you made for yourself. You've named the proxy to act on your behalf, but this decision you have made already and this clearly sets forth your wishes when it comes to that.

The other thing that the living Will does is it helps minimize the "guilt factor" when it comes to your health care proxy having to make a decision about sustaining your life by these artificial means. Oftentimes, family members or health care proxies are stricken with guilt about whether or not to shut those machines off ("pull the plug") either because they're unclear about what you wanted or their own personal beliefs, religious or otherwise, may get in the way. Having this living Will expresses your wishes clearly to your health care proxy and, therefore, they don't have to feel guilty about letting you pass away peacefully by shutting the machines off, because that document clearly tells the medical providers and the health care proxy and the other family members what you want. It takes away the potential for arguments between family members who may disagree over whether or not you would want to be kept alive in this way. It clearly delineates the decision that you made for yourself.

Another document that goes hand in hand with the health care proxy is what's called a HIPAA waiver. HIPAA stands for the Health Insurance Portability and Accountability Act, which is a US law designed to provide privacy standards to protect patients' medical records and other health information. The HIPAA rules deal with privacy, specifically, your right to privacy with regard to your medical records and to whom and what your doctors can release to anyone other than you. You are supposed to have the right to privacy and control over your medical records and have the right to keep those records confidential so that they cannot be shared. Yet, there may become instances when you want or need those records to be shared with your health care proxy because the record information may be relevant to a decision that your health care proxy needs to make on your behalf.

HIPAA puts your medical providers in a tight corner because there's no real exception in the HIPAA rules that automatically allow them to speak to a health care proxy about your past medical situation and records. There's nothing in the rules right now that say the health care proxy is exempt from these privacy rules. Even doctors often won't know what to do, and can certainly be afraid to have these discussions with your health care proxy, for fear of violating HIPAA.

What we do is we have clients sign what's called a HIPAA waiver. It's a document that goes along with your health care proxy. It clearly states to your medical providers that they have the right to discuss your medical situation, your medical history, and your medical records with your health care proxy. It takes away any potential privacy issue that your medical providers may have and tells them clearly that they are authorized to speak to your health care proxy about your health and about the decisions to be made. The HIPAA waiver goes for your primary health care proxy, and for the backup proxies named in that document as well, so that it's clearly stated to your physicians that they have no cause for concern about the HIPAA rules when discussing your medical history and situation with your health care proxies.

Let's now look at one additional document that, while is certainly optional, goes along with the health care proxy, and is somewhat similar to what's contemplated with a living Will. As we discussed, the living Will deals with being kept alive on machines, such as respirators or feeding tubes. There are situations where clients might want to make their wishes known in case they were ever to suffer from either advanced stages of dementia or Alzheimer's, or other types of diseases where the client can't make informed decisions about their health care, and specifically in situations where that client can no longer feed themselves.

An important thing to consider when working through your estate plan provisions is for the client to think about what to do if they can't feed themselves. Do they want their caregivers to basically force them to eat? Or, if they get to the point where their Alzheimer's or dementia is so advanced that they forget how to eat, they can't eat, they don't want to eat, or they will fight if feeding is attempted, then they may not want their care providers to force-feed them in that way. And knowing that the result is going to be their eventual passing from not being able to eat, many still decide that they don't want to be force-fed, which can often be very traumatic to someone suffering from Alzheimer's and dementia because they don't really understand what's going on. They don't have the capacity to understand and suffer extreme fear and discomfort with someone forcing food or water into their mouths.

We offer documentation where clients can express their wishes. Again, while they're filling out these documents, we're talking about dealing with healthy, lucid people with sufficient mental capacity to make these types of decisions to be utilized and reviewed in the event that they lose that capacity, or they're suffering from Alzheimer's or dementia, and can't make these decisions anymore. The documentation can include preferences with regard to administering (or not administering) medications, whether or not they want to continue to have medications given to them, or whether they want their medication to be withdrawn. They can deal with whether or not they want to be force-fed. In other words, if they'll no longer accept hand-feeding, do they want to be fed by a feeding tube? They can also express their wishes with regard to their hygiene, how they want to be treated, and things like moisturizing the lips and mouth and gums to avoid discomfort. These documents also contemplate the potential application of medication to relieve suffering and relieve pain, even though these medications might shorten life. Wishes can also be expressed as to end of life decisions, where the individual can state that they would prefer to die at home if possible, but if not, they would want to go to an institution that will respect their wishes set out in these documents.

CHAPTER 7

A WORD ABOUT GRAY AREAS

All of these Big Three documents, and especially some of these health care documents, are designed to minimize gray areas. As an attorney that drafts these type of documents for people, I hate gray areas. I like for a document to contemplate as many potential situations as possible and provide answers for those situations. When I have to review documents that other attorneys may have drafted or that clients may have drafted on their own through assistance of some type of online platform, one of the things that I'm looking for in determining whether or not a document is a good document is a gray area.

It's often my job to look at the worst-case scenario when reviewing documents that clients bring to me. I look at these documents and try and figure out if there's some way that either (1) your wants or wishes could be misconstrued, (2) there is some place where your wants or wishes are simply absent, or (3) there is any place that could cause another individual, be it a family member, a friend, or a medical institution or a financial institution, to have trouble deciphering your wishes. We draft our documents to be crystal clear, and eliminate as much gray area as possible so that, within the four corners of that document, any other person or institution could look at that document and find the answer to their question, find the answer to what it is you wanted, or find what you were trying to express. We want all those answers to be in the document itself, free from confusion and alternative interpretations.

We know that it's not possible to eliminate all gray areas because what we're doing is we're signing documents that are going to be used in the future and none of us know what type of situation could come up in the future with regard to your health, with regard to your financial well-being, and with regard to your family, changes in life, and life events. So, we use our best efforts to design our documents to withstand the test of time as much as possible, contemplate life changes, and also to keep things clear and answer any questions that anyone would have. We want that document to be able to deal with as many potential issues as possible, even though there's no way to deal with them all. We try to eliminate these gray areas so that there's no question about what to do.

We want a client to be able to give their estate planning documents to their family members or their dedicated individuals with confidence that their wishes are going to be followed, with no ambiguity. Oftentimes, we're asked to review documents, again, either drafted by other attorneys, or drafted years ago, or drafted through an online portal and I get a power of attorney or a health care proxy that's one or two pages long. And I know, just from the very fact that the document is so short, that it's not going to be able to contemplate the myriad of potential situations that could materialize down the road. With a two- to three-page document, even before my review, I am aware right away, as soon as I receive a document of that length, that it's going to need to be redone.

CHAPTER 8

WHAT IS A TRUST AND HOW CAN A TRUST HELP YOU?

In addition to those Big Three documents that we talked about that form the basis for any estate plan, there is one other type of document that follows closely behind the trio, and that is the trust. We get lots of questions about trusts and whether or not a trust might be helpful. There are different types of trusts, with different names, provisions, and purposes. A confusing thing about trusts is that we use different names and terms for the same trust. It can be very confusing, especially when clients go online and try to research matters on their own, as they may be seeing a trust that goes by one name on one webpage, then a different webpage uses a different name, and they don't realize that they're talking about the same type of trust. For all the good that Google does for the world, at times it can be an attorney's worst enemy, because the client gets mixed up with inaccurate or outdated information.

There are lots of different types of trusts. We will go over the four primary types of trusts that we use in our estate planning practice, which are each utilized depending on the individual client's situation. Once again, we look at each individual client on a case-by-case basis, and determine (1) whether you even need a trust and (2) if it is worth the extra money and time to put a trust together. If so, what type of trust is going to work for you? We don't like to add documents to an estate plan unless they provide genuine value, and we therefore only recommend trusts if they are really needed.

First, let's talk about what a trust is, because people often get confused about what exactly a trust is and why it could be helpful. The concept of a trust is to create an entity that acts almost like a business or almost like another living person. It holds assets for the benefit of somebody else. There can be lots of different reasons for creating a trust and putting someone called a "trustee" in charge of certain assets for the benefit of someone else. The person that creates the trust is usually referred to either as a donor or a trustor. The trust also has to have what's called a trustee, and the trustee is the person who is responsible for holding the trust assets, handling the day-to-day requirements of the trust, and making distributions from the trust that are in the beneficiary's best interest. The trustee is responsible for protecting the assets in the trust, dispersing the assets in the trust, and filing tax returns for the trust if tax returns are necessary. The trust creates a fiduciary duty (there's that phrase again!) owed by the trustee to the beneficiary. Note that the donor and the trustee can sometimes be the same person. In fact, very often they are.

Now we know what the trustee does, so let's talk about the other person or entity that is involved with a trust, the beneficiary or beneficiaries. A beneficiary is the person or entity that the trust funds are being held for the benefit of. If I want to, for example, set up a trust for my kids, I may be the donor or trustor because I'm going to put assets aside into this trust for the benefit of my children. I could do this by a present transfer of those assets, or I could do it through my Will at the time of my passing. The children are the beneficiaries, and then I have to name a trustee who will be responsible for following the rules of the trust. That trustee might be myself during my lifetime and I may have a backup person named who will take over as trustee if I were to pass away. In a situation like that, I'm both the donor and the trustee, yet I've named other beneficiaries. In other words, that trust is for the benefit of someone else, in that example, my kids. I do have such a trust in my own estate plan.

A trust is almost like a Will in the respect that it contains a list of instructions. Just like your personal representative has to follow the instructions in your Will, the trustee has to follow the instructions in the trust. In other words, we're not looking for the trustee to have complete freedom in their actions, or have the ability to deal with trust assets however they feel like it. The trustee is bound by the trust document, the four corners of the trust document, and is required, per their fiduciary duty, to follow the instructions in that trust document. This is another situation where, once again, we are trying to be crystal clear about what the trustee can do, what the trustee can't do, and eliminate or minimize as much as we can the gray areas. We need the trustee, especially in a case where the donor, the creator of the trust, may have passed away, to be able to look at that document, and its verbiage, and be able to have any question in their head answered by that verbiage. We don't need the trustee to ever have to wonder or think about what the donor may have wanted, what the donor's intent was, or what the donor wanted to see happen when they passed. We want all that information to be included in the trust document itself.

The concept of including as many possible scenarios in the trust document is yet another reason why we don't like software-derived documents. Drafting a trust for yourself online creates a document that meets the minimum legal requirements (sometimes not even that!) and doesn't consider your specific needs or situation. A lawyer-drafted trust, when done properly, takes these factors into consideration and modifies the trust draft accordingly. Make no mistake, lawyers do not reinvent the wheel every time, and they may use the same base draft, but a good lawyer will tweak and modify that base draft to fit the client's specific needs. That's the part that is missing from software-drafted or online-drafted documents.

In our practice, we have four types of trusts that are used most often:

The revocable family trust

The credit shelter trust

The life insurance trust

The irrevocable Medicaid income only trust

The most common type of trust that we use in the office is often called a family trust. It's also sometimes called an inter vivos trust or a probate-avoidance trust. This type of trust, generally, is what we call fully revocable. What that means is that the donor, the creator of the trust, maintains for themselves the right to alter and amend that trust at any time. And there are reasons why some trusts are revocable and some trusts are irrevocable, and irrevocable trusts cannot be changed. There are reasons and benefits for doing irrevocable trusts that we will get into later.

For now, let's stick with talking about a revocable family trust or inter vivos trust. We most commonly use these types of trusts when we're doing an estate plan for a client that has young children. The point of the family trust is to protect money that a client wants to leave for his/her children, but the children are too young to inherit those assets on their own. In this type of situation, we'll set up what's called a "pour-over Will" for the client, where the personal representative's duty, under that Will, is to convey the probate assets to this family trust. And at that point, those assets come under the control of the trustee. Setting the estate plan up in this manner allows for long-term control over the assets, versus a single, one-time distribution to beneficiaries under the Will. Instead, the terms of the trust are the controlling factor, and can provide for long-term retention of assets and specific distributions as per the trust provisions. The trust can be crafted so as to allow for more flexibility and control over the assets.

In the pour-over Will scenario, the personal rep. and the trustee are occasionally the same person, which is perfectly fine. It's a matter of personal choice, but there's no rule against the designated person named as personal rep. also serving as the trustee of the trust. In fact, it can often be more convenient to structure it that way.

The trusts we draft have clear and concise directions with regard to the power and authority of the trustee, and how the trust funds are to be collected, held, and distributed. What we then do is we set out rules for this trustee and how that trustee needs to administer the funds on behalf of the beneficiaries. The trust provisions are designed on a case-by-case basis and one factor we consider is how much discretion we want the trustee to have. In some cases, we may want the trustee to have very little discretion, where the donor clearly spells out what exactly is to happen with the assets, and in other cases we may leave some of the decision-making to the trustee's discretion, where they can determine whether or not they want to, or need to, make a certain distribution to the beneficiary. Most trusts are in the middle, where there are some specific provisions, such as benchmark ages where distributions are required to be made, but discretionary distributions by the trustee prior to those benchmark ages, where the trustee decides what is in the best interest of the beneficiaries.

There are a number of benefits to a revocable family trust. A primary benefit is control over the funds for the benefit of your young children. If you have a young child that's inheriting money from an estate, that child's too young to control the money for themselves. What's going to happen, without a trust, is control of those funds will go to that child's guardian. There are many reasons why we may or may not want the guardian to have any control over money that you leave to a child. When money is left to a guardian in that way, there is no oversight. There are no rules, and there's nothing controlling the way that money can be used. It's completely and 100 percent up to the guardian to determine what they want to do with the funds, and there's no stopping them from converting funds for their own use, whereas, with a trust, we have set parameters to ensure that the assets are to be used for the benefit of the beneficiaries, which in this case would be your child.

When we leave money to a child without a trust, and control rests in the guardian, the guardian can go out and buy themselves a new sports car, or use the money for their own kids' college educations, even though that money belongs to your children. While we want to think that anyone we would name as guardian wouldn't use the money in that way, there's really no way to predict what anyone is capable of in a desperate situation. When we leave money to a trust, the trustee is bound by the terms of the trust to do what the trust says and use the assets for the benefit of the beneficiaries. What we often do is set up a trust for clients that have young children. We name a trustee. The trustee will administer the money on behalf of the children, and usually what we do is give the trustee discretion to make discretionary disbursements to that child if the trustee determines that they're needed. But at all times, the trustee's fiduciary duty is to the beneficiaries.

If the trustee wants to use the money to purchase something for the beneficiary, something the beneficiary needs, the trust provides for this—for example, school supplies, extracurricular activities, and entertainment. Or maybe the beneficiary needs a car to drive to school. Well, that's a discretionary decision made by the trustee, who has the authority to determine whether or not they want to make a disbursement like that, and possibly talk the child into a Honda instead of a Corvette. If the child needs money for health care, or if the child needs money to go to college, the trustee makes those decisions in their discretion. That's why it's really important to think about and consider carefully who you want to be the trustee. It's called a trust for a reason. You're putting great faith and trust into the individual that you're naming to be the trustee. And that's why it's called a trust in the first place.

The way that we commonly set these trusts up is to allow discretionary spending by the trustee, but we also build in certain time periods or ages when the trustee distributes some of the money to the beneficiaries. Oftentimes, we'll use benchmark ages, such as giving a third of what's in the trust to a beneficiary when they're twenty, the other third when they're twenty-five, and the remaining third when they're thirty. But they can be any ages that the client uses. I have clients that will tell me their children are pretty responsible with money, so they can have their disbursements earlier, and I also have clients who tell me their kids can't be trusted with the funds until they are fifty! And in the meantime, the trustee can utilize discretionary spending in between, so it's not as if the beneficiary doesn't have any money during those periods. But what we're trying to avoid is giving a huge lump-sum of money to a young person. If we've got someone that's eighteen or twenty-one years old inheriting a whole bunch of money, we don't really know that that individual is going to be responsible with that money; therefore, we spread out the distributions over time so that the individual isn't receiving a large sum all at once that they can go spend. Prior to these set distribution ages, the trustee can always use discretionary funds to cover any normal expenses and potential shortfalls.

Another provision that we use in our trusts deals with trustee discretion in situations where it might be better to withhold distributions from the beneficiary, which can be important for several reasons. A trustee can decide to withhold distributions at certain times if they determine it's in the best interest of the beneficiary. For example, if the beneficiary is applying to college and is applying for financial aid, we may not want the trustee to make a big distribution to that beneficiary and put all kinds of money in the bank because then that beneficiary isn't going to qualify for any financial aid because they own these assets. So the trustee has discretion in the trust that we use to withhold making a distribution until the financial aid period has passed. And that way, it won't adversely affect the financial aid application.

Another example would be if the beneficiary is receiving any type of government benefits, whether it's for health care or other types of government benefits, such as housing. Some of those benefits are what's called asset-based. What that means is if you own over a certain amount of assets, you can't qualify. And maybe we've got a beneficiary that qualifies, but if we give them a distribution out of the trust, they're not going to qualify anymore. And the trustee can look at that situation and use their discretion to determine that they want to wait on a distribution so that it does not disrupt benefits being received by the beneficiary or make a beneficiary ineligible for benefits.

A third situation that the trustee can use discretion for is if they think that giving a distribution to a beneficiary would have a negative effect on that beneficiary's health, such as, if a beneficiary were having problems with addiction or seeking treatment for addiction. That's definitely not a time where you want to give a large influx of money to a beneficiary. We give the trustee the authority to hold back from making those distributions directly to a beneficiary because we'd be afraid that beneficiary could use the money to fuel their addiction. Even while withholding distributions directly to the child, the trustee can still make discretionary payments to service providers and pay other individuals, but maybe refrain from making payments directly over to the beneficiary in that type of health-related situation.

Our trusts also include some authority for a trustee to put funds into what we call a "supplemental needs trust," where we may have a child that's receiving some government benefits and we want to use the money to supplement those benefits but not make the child ineligible for those benefits. A supplemental needs trust is a very specific type of trust that deals with using money in such a way that it won't make the child ineligible for benefits. We make sure our family trusts have this option built-in.

As I mentioned, the majority of the time we make these family trusts fully revocable. Quite often, we don't fund these trusts during our lifetimes. In other words, we create the trust, and the trust exists, but we don't put any money in there during the client's lifetime. These family trusts are considered to be emergency measures. If Mom and Dad were to pass away suddenly, this trust comes into being and holds assets for the benefit of the children, and those assets enter the trust through the pour-over Will. But, while Mom and Dad are good and fine and healthy, there's usually no need to have money in these trusts.

To make this work, the Will leaves the client's probate assets to the trust. The trust can also be the beneficiary of life insurance proceeds and other types of financial instruments. We make the trust the beneficiary of these various types of accounts or insurance policies. Then if the client were to pass away, those funds pour over into the trust. But, because the trust is fully revocable, the donor reserves unto themselves the right to change this trust, amend it at any time, tear it up, and throw it away at any time. It's flexible in that it can be changed as much or as little as the donor wants.

When drafting, we reserve that right to alter and amend solely to the donors. In other words, once the donors pass away, and if Mom and Dad are the donors and they create this trust and they pass away, the revocability of the trust changes. At that point, it's no longer revocable. We reserve that right to revoke the trust only to the original donor. If Mom and Dad pass away, and they name a sibling, cousin, brother, whomever as the trustee, that trustee no longer has the right to revoke or amend the trust. That way, we don't have to worry about the trustee making changes to the trust that the donors didn't intend. Only the donors have the right to alter or amend the trust. The successor trustees don't have those rights and, therefore, the successor trustees are bound by the wishes as stated in the document that the donors put together in the first place.

The trustee, while acting in that capacity, is bound by a fiduciary duty. What that means is that by law, the trustee must act in the best interest of the beneficiary. It means they're not supposed to take the money out and use it on themselves. They're not supposed to use the money for the benefit of anybody other than the beneficiaries. And to do otherwise is a violation of their fiduciary duty, which is a very, very serious thing that has legal consequences.

CHAPTER 9

USING TRUSTS FOR ESTATE TAX SAVINGS

We've now talked about revocable trusts for children and the various reasons and benefits of that type of trust. There are numerous other types of trusts that all provide various other benefits, each with their own rules, and there are a variety of different reasons for using these trusts.

There are other types of trust beyond the family trust, from our list above. These other trusts have other purposes, one of which is to help avoid or reduce estate taxes. Our estate plans utilize two different types of trusts when we're talking about estate taxes: the life insurance trust and the credit shelter trust.

If I told you I could save you **$64,000** in taxes, would it be worth it to you?

What about if I could save you **$82,000** in taxes? Now is it worth it?

Would it be worth it to you to spend a much smaller up-front cost, and save that kind of money? Yes? Then read on.

Do you want to pay estate taxes? No? Well if you haven't planned, you might be paying them anyway.

When you made your Will, did you leave any money to the government? No way, right? You might be wrong about that. Most of us don't want to leave any money to the government in our estate plans. We've given them plenty already, paying our income taxes every year, as well as all the other taxes we pay.

We want to leave our money to our families. What if I told you that the government might very well be one of your beneficiaries, and you don't even know it? Would you do something about it? If so, then you're smart. But most people don't.

If you don't do anything, it's exactly the same as if you named the government as a beneficiary in your Will, to inherit your money. Why? Because of Estate Taxes.

Is estate tax only paid by millionaires? Nope. It's paid by regular folks, who pay it because they haven't planned, never realized they'd have to pay it, and chose not to educate themselves. They took no action. Do the opposite – take action. Fix the problem.

First of all, what are estate taxes? Here in Massachusetts, our estates have to contend with two types of tax, federal and state. We can be subject to a federal estate tax; however, that threshold recently went way, way up, and in 2019 the federal estate tax only affects the top 1 percent of Americans. A decedent's taxable estate has to include assets of at least $5.6 million for an individual, and a married couple will only be subject to federal estate tax if they have assets over $11.2 million. However, in Massachusetts, there is also a state level estate tax. The estate tax threshold in Massachusetts is $1,000,000,(in 2019) much, much lower than the federal limit.

Most people, and most clients, obviously aren't millionaires. They don't have $1,000,000 in the bank, so they think they don't have to worry about the Massachusetts estate tax. However, what people don't often realize is that things like life insurance proceeds can be includable in the calculation of your taxable estate assets. Even if life insurance has direct beneficiaries, and isn't considered a probate asset, it absolutely can still be included in your taxable estate. While a client might not have $1,000,000 in the bank, he/she might have some money in the bank. She might own a home, and there's some equity there that has value. She might have some retirement accounts and there's equity there that has value. And then there's life insurance. All of these assets added together can put the taxable estate over the limit. Many clients of ours, especially parents of young kids, often have life insurance policies of $500,000 or more, even $1,000,000, or $1,500,000, because they're trying to provide for their families and children if they were to pass away. Well, if you have a life insurance policy of $1,000,000, then that $1,000,000, if you're not careful, can be included in your taxable estate and can put you over the $1,000,000 threshold and make you responsible for some Massachusetts estate taxes. Without planning, estates reaching $2,000,000 can pay roughly $82,000 in estate taxes!

Clients can be over that $1,000,000 limit without even realizing it because people think that, "my life insurance goes directly to my beneficiary. It doesn't go through probate; it's not a probate asset." And people often confuse probate asset with the taxable estate. Just because an asset isn't a probate asset, and it isn't part of your probate and goes directly to a beneficiary, doesn't mean it's not taxable. Taxes have their own rules, and a probate estate is very different from a taxable estate. The federal government and state government don't want you to realize this, because if you don't plan, the governments get paid in tax dollars from your estate. So we have to be cognizant that, even though they're not probate assets, they can still be includable in your taxable estate. This misconception leads to people thinking they're below the threshold and they're actually over it.

When we have a client that is potentially over the threshold, the next thing we look at is why. What's putting them over the threshold? Is it their money in the bank or other assets that they own? Or is it simply life insurance that puts them over that $1,000,000 limit? In other words, if not for the life insurance, they would be under the cap. In cases where we determine that the life insurance is the "culprit" that puts the client over the $1,000,000 threshold, we look at ways to potentially bring them back below that threshold. And we use another type of trust to do that, and that type of trust is called an irrevocable life insurance trust, or ILIT (eye-lit).

If done properly, you can have your life insurance owned by a life insurance trust. Once that life insurance trust is in existence, that life insurance, if you die, is payable to the trust and then, through the trust, is payable to the trust beneficiaries, which may be the same people you were going to leave that life insurance to anyway. However, because it's in that irrevocable life insurance trust when the irrevocable life insurance trust receives the proceeds, they're payable through the trust to the beneficiaries, but because of that irrevocable trust, that money can be excluded from your taxable estate. It's very important to note that this has to be an irrevocable trust, which means it can't be changed. Irrevocable trusts get a bad rap, because people fear the inability to make edits. But it takes that irrevocability factor that makes the trustor just "hands off" enough for the government to consider the trust the owner of that policy and not the trustor as the owner. When used correctly, there's no need to fear the fact that the trust is irrevocable. If you change your mind, and can't change the trust, then you simply don't fund that trust by changing the life insurance instead. As another logistical note, there's a difference between transferring an existing life insurance policy to an ILIT versus having the ILIT purchase a new policy. If you are transferring an existing life insurance policy into the ILIT, you have to live for three years after the transfer. Then the proceeds will pass outside your estate. If instead, you're taking out a new life insurance policy with the trust as purchaser and owner, there is no three-year time requirement. There are yearly requirements with regard to notifications to beneficiaries (legally referred to as Crummey notices, named after the famous case where the ILIT was first recognized by the IRS) but the notices are fairly simple to do. Once those yearly requirements are met, those funds are excludable from the taxable estate. Therefore, if the life insurance was the culprit that was going to put our client over the threshold, they can be brought back down below that threshold because we've excluded the life insurance, and saved a ton of dough on estate tax. In other cases, we've got clients that might be over the $1,000,000 threshold because of other types of assets, where the life insurance may only play a small part or no part, and they've got cash assets or equity assets, namely real estate, that puts them over the $1,000,000 threshold. And we look at ways to try and reduce or eliminate estate taxes through other types of trusts that don't deal specifically with life insurance.

For married couples, the type of trust that we often use is what's called a credit shelter trust. What the credit shelter trust is designed to do is to take advantage of every individual's $1,000,000 threshold. Every person is entitled to pass away with $1,000,000 in assets, without paying estate tax. But most married couples own their assets jointly, or leave everything to their spouse in their Will, and what happens is that first spouse to pass away has no taxable estate. Thus, their $1,000,000 exemption is essentially lost, and all of the joint assets are part of the surviving spouse's estate, who then pays heavy estate tax at time of death. The credit shelter trust is designed to ensure that each spouse gets their maximum $1,000,000 exemption by allowing $1,000,000 in assets to be in the first spouse's taxable estate, and then be excluded from the surviving spouse's estate. So, if we've got a married couple that has over $1,000,000 worth of assets and one of the spouses passes away but maybe only had $500,000 of assets solely in their name, then without planning, they can only use $500,000 of their $1,000,000 exemption, but the other $500,000 in exemptions can be lost.

What the credit shelter trust is designed to do is to make sure both spouses get the maximum $1,000,000 exemption amount. If one spouse passes away, we look at the assets in that client's name and we position assets ahead of time, during their lifetime, to set this up so that it happens properly. We set up the trust to basically make two new sub-trusts for the surviving spouse, one of which holds the $1,000,000 exemption amount, which is the first $1,000,000 to keep the deceased person's estate under the threshold. Thus, there's no tax there because that sub-trust holds $1,000,000 and it's not over the limit. Because it's not over the limit, there's no tax. And then, we make sure that the trust provisions allow access by the surviving spouse to that $1,000,000, and those disbursements are at the trustee's discretion; therefore, they're not included in the surviving spouse's estate.

It sounds complicated, and it's more difficult to describe than it is to put it in practice. We show some examples to our clients about how the credit shelter trust can make a difference in estate taxes. We'll list three or four examples (see below) that will illustrate exactly how it works and how you can save a lot of money, in some cases nearly $100,000 in tax savings, of what could be potential estate taxes that we avoid by doing one of these credit shelter trusts.

EXAMPLES:

If we don't do any planning in a case where Spouse#1 and Spouse#2 have $1.5 million and the Spouse#1 leaves everything to Spouse#2 at death, then Spouse#2, who inherited everything when Spouse#1 passed away, later dies with $1.5 million in his/her taxable estate. Spouse#2's taxable estate would be over the limit and in 2019 figures, she would owe Massachusetts estate taxes of around $64,000.

If we utilize a credit shelter trust, Spouse#1 and Spouse#2 split their $1.5 million evenly, and can hold them in these trusts with credit shelter trust provisions. If Spouse#1 dies, and we use the trust, his $750,000 in assets is below the estate tax limit, so there is no estate tax to pay. Then, Spouse#1's half is available to Spouse#2 through the trust, but is excluded from his/her taxable estate. If Spouse#2 later passes away, his/her taxable estate consists of the $750,000 in his/her assets, which is under the limit, and Spouse#1's $750,000 in the credit shelter trust is under the limit, so no estate taxes are due, saving $64,000!

The same principles apply to a larger estate. Let's look at a situation where the married couple has $3,000,000 in assets. If we don't do any planning, and Spouse#1 dies, withSpouse#2 inheriting everything, then Spouse#2 now has the full $3,000,000 in her taxable estate. If Spouse#2 passes away, she is over the $1,000,000 limit by $2,000,000, and her estate would owe a Massachusetts estate tax of around $182,000. Big bucks!

Using the credit shelter trust, we have the couple split their assets evenly. If Spouse#1 dies, we put $1,000,000 into the credit shelter trust, where (1) it's under the limit for estate taxes, and (2) it's still available to Spouse#2 during his/her lifetime but excludable from her estate. The other $500,000 from Spouse#1's half of the total assets is put into a separate trust, called a marital deduction trust. The marital deduction trust funds are also available to Spouse#2, though they are still included in her taxable estate. Later, when Spouse#2 passes away, her estate taxable estate includes her original half of the assets, at $1,500,000 plus the $500,000 in the marital trust (the $1.000,000 in the credit shelter trust is excluded), for a total estate of $2,000,000. Spouse#2 would be over the Massachusetts estate tax limit by $1,000,000 (instead of being over by $2,000,000 in the example without planning). Spouse#2 would owe a Massachusetts estate tax of around $100,000, instead of the $182,000 in our example of non- planning. That's an estate tax savings of $82,000! Now, isn't an $82,000 savings worth it?

That's why a qualified, experienced estate planning attorney can really save the day! The government doesn't want you to do this. They want you to use software and online tools that don't take advantage of the tax laws, and don't position you to save taxes. Your estate planning lawyer looks out for you. Spending some money on an experienced attorney now can save you many, many thousands later.

The last major type of trust that we use here in our office is what's called a Medicaid irrevocable income-only trust, or Medicaid rust for short. This one is a little more complicated. The purpose is to protect assets for our clients when the client, or their parents, are preparing to receive long-term care or move into a nursing home. We'll reserve discussion of the Medicaid trust for our elder law section, later. We'll delve into the reasons behind utilizing a Medicaid trust, what the benefits are, what the drawbacks are, and how they really can help protect the assets of an individual that's going into long-term care.

CHAPTER 10

A FEW WORDS ABOUT GUARDIANSHIPS

GUARDIANSHIPS, PUT SIMPLY, are the naming of individuals to take care of the children of someone who has either passed away or become incapacitated. Clients wonder what's going to happen to their children if they were to pass away, or suffer from a health problem that affects their ability to care for their kids. So if Mom and Dad pass away, or become incapacitated, now what? Well, in the absence of documentation detailing the parents' guardianship nominations, it's up to a family member or friend or another individual that's close to the children to petition the court for guardianship and explain to the court why they would be the best person to take care of the children and raise the children. Guardianships are accomplished with a probate filing, or a probate petition, where an attorney generally has to be involved. It can be time-consuming. It can be expensive. And what we try and do in our documents is put a plan in place for guardianship of the clients' children, and as usual, while trying to make things crystal clear and not leave any gray areas.

We accomplish the guardianship nominations in two different ways. The first is through the last Will and Testament, as mentioned in our chapter on Wills. Your last Will and testament can include provisions where you name who you would want to be the guardian of your children if both parents of the child were to pass away. It's a good idea to name at least one backup person to the guardians, again, in the event that the guardians are unable to do it or can't do it or are pre-deceased by the client. These provisions in the Will are used so that the parents' wishes are clear and without ambiguity. If a married couple is nominated for guardianship, we can go further and state the preferences if the couple were to separate or divorce.

But remember, a last Will and testament has no legal significance during a person's lifetime. It's not "written in stone" until the testator passes away. That's because every individual has the right to change their Will—tear it up, throw it away, alter it, or amend it—any time they want to while they're alive. Therefore, a Will isn't legally binding until the person dies.

So, what happens if someone becomes incapacitated, such is in a car accident or from having a stroke? Sure, we've got a guardian nominated in the Will for when the person passes away, but what if the person is still alive? What if the person is still alive but becomes incapacitated, is in a coma, or is in the hospital? Well, we can't look to the Will for guardianship of that person's children because the Will has no legal significance because the person is still alive. They may be comatose. They may be otherwise disabled. But the Will doesn't carry any weight.

The way we handle that in our estate plans is to draft a separate guardianship document where the client clearly expresses what happens if they become incapacitated. The concept is, "Well, if I'm dead, you can look to my Will. My Will says who the guardian should be. But, if I'm not dead, I'm alive, but I'm incapacitated, I'm in a coma, whatever the case may be, I name guardians to take care of my children in that instance." That avoids any question about who in the family should be the guardian, and leaves no ambiguity about who should be applying for guardianship through the court. The courts certainly still have to be involved, but you've got a much more open-and-shut probate case or petition when guardianship is clearly established by these documents.

That's why our estate plans establish guardianship in two different ways. One through the Will, and one through separate guardianship nomination documents that deal with incapacitation only.

PART II

ELDER LAW

INTRODUCTION TO ELDER LAW

Now let's move into a discussion of the field of elder law. First of all, I hate that name because it conjures up an image of people that are old and frail, and not lucid, and don't know what's going on. I hate that the field of law is referred to like that, as elder law or elder care law. Really, the biggest thing and most important point when it comes to elder law has to do with planning early, or planning before you get to the point where you're so far advanced in years that you're not as lucid or competent as you were before. Elder law usually starts long before you're an "elder." The ideal client that comes to see me about elder law is in their fifties. That's the best time to start planning.

The reason for that is because many of our planning techniques require time to pass in order for them to become effective. There are lots of details that go along with elder law, including positioning of assets in a certain way that it allows an individual to be eligible for long-term care benefits. Those types of asset transfers carry a time frame with them and if those asset transfers aren't made early enough, then those asset transfers can bring about a penalty period when it comes to applyingto Medicaid forlong-term care benefits. We'll get more into that.

CHAPTER 1

HOW TO CHOOSE AN ELDER LAW ATTORNEY

First of all, what should you look for in an elder law attorney? This is a field of law that is very specialized. You need to find an attorney that focuses their practice on elder law. It can be very damaging to have work done by an attorney that just dabbles in that area of practice. Attorneys without the right training can negatively impact you in ways that are very difficult to repair, especially if you wait too long. So that's quality number one in an elder lawyer—focus of practice on that field of law.

The second thing you need to look for is an attorney that regularly attends continuing education on elder law. Elder law is in a constant state of flux. Rules and laws change all the time, based on the government, and based on Congress, because those entities control and provide the benefits for many of our elders. In order to help you position yourself to be eligible for those benefits, an attorney needs to be up to date on the rules and the changing landscape. You need to hire an attorney that is attending continuing education in that field regularly, so that they are always up on new cases and new trends. Document provisions that work today aren't necessarily going to work tomorrow, and continuing education is the only way to stay current.

The next attribute that you want to look for is an attorney that has some experience. I'm not one to ever knock a brand new law school graduate. I was a new law school graduate myself at one time (many moons ago!). Someone that's brand new just out of school, in my opinion, isn't the right fit for this type of practice. This field, this highly specialized field, is one where you should hire someone that has some experience and has been practicing in estate planning for a little while and then moved on to elder law. That's the natural progression for having proficiency in this area, and that progression takes time.

Next, when it comes to choosing an elder law attorney, you want to select someone that is not stingy with their information. Look at the attorney's website, call the attorney's office, and see what information they're willing to give you. Do they have free information that's downloadable or viewable on their website? Are they willing to mail you any information that they're able to send you for free? Have they written articles, reports, or other publications that they can send to you? Good attorneys, attorneys that do this work well, make enough money that they can afford to send you some information. The hope may be that you eventually come in and become a client, but they should be able to send you information without any obligation and at the same time have a website that allows you to view or download information and not have it cost you anything.

Lastly, you want an attorney that won't hand you a set of documents and disappear. A good attorney is going to stay in contact with you after your documents are signed. Staying in contact can be through emails, cards, and newsletters. That way, you can be assured that your attorney is going to contact you in the event of a law change or other rule change that could affect your planning.

CHAPTER 2

THE THREE BASIC TYPES OF ELDER LAW CLIENTS

When is it time to consult with an elder law attorney? What's the right age to start looking into this? Elder law clients tend to come in one of three forms. The first type is the client that's in their late forties or early fifties, when it's much too soon for them to have an immediate concern about their long-term care, but they know that it's an eventuality and that long-term care is out there looming. The smart clients, the ones that plan ahead, are looking to position themselves in the best way so that they're ready for it. That's client type number one, and they are the ones in the best position to consult with an elder lawyer.

The second client type makes up other ways that elder law clients tend to originate, which is through the elder's children. We very frequently receive calls from a potential client's adult kids, kids in their forties or even fifties whose parents are getting on in years and have to start thinking about a plan for long-term care. These clients' needs might be slightly different than client type number one, because they may be preparing to enter long-term care relatively soon, within the next few years.

The third and final type of client that comes in for elder care, whether it's the clients themselves or their children, is for what's called crisis planning. Crisis planning is when the client is either in the nursing home already or is planning to enter the nursing home immediately. These clients have not pre-planned for their long-term care and now are in a position where they're either in immediate need of long-term care or even entering a long-term care facility and are trying to make last-minute moves in order to protect assets and qualify for benefits. The crisis planning is a sad situation because I'm often stuck telling clients that if they had just come to see me a few years earlier, there would've been a lot more options available at the time. That doesn't mean that we can't help a client with crisis planning, but you're generally able to protect much more in the amount of assets and offer a lot more options when clients come in sooner and not wait until the crisis point.

CHAPTER 3

LONG-TERM CARE

MOST ELDER LAW work has to do with planning for long-term care. Long-term care can mean any number of things. Long-term care is care that can take place in the home and it is care that can be done in a facility. Long-term care can refer to assisted living, and it can refer to nursing homes. But it can also refer to in-home services that are designed to keep an individual in their home longer. In-home services are services that, because they're being provided in the home, can prevent an individual from having to move into a facility much sooner. When it comes to long-term care, whether we're talking about in-home care or nursing home care, there are basically three ways to pay. The first way is to self-pay. You use your money to pay for your care and you continue to use that money to pay for your care for the duration of your life, or until your money is gone. This is the least desirable of the options, and much of the planning that we do is designed to specifically avoid this, by putting certain legal documents and vehicles in place to protect assets.

The second way to pay for long-term care is through a long-term care insurance policy and there are two different types. There's traditional long-term care insurance, sometimes called

LTC insurance. That insurance is designed to pay for some or all of your long-term care, whether that long-term care occurs at a facility or occurs in the home. Typically, there are two types of policy limits for LTC insurance. There's a policy limit on how much can be paid monthly, where the policy has a maximum monthly benefit and after that monthly benefit, the remaining balance toward any long-term care has to come from another source, such as self-pay. The other policy limit to a long-term care insurance policy is an overall lifetime policy limit. A policy may allow you a certain amount per month, but there is also an overall policy limit, and once benefits are paid out and that coverage limit is reached, the policy is maxed out and isn't going to pay anymore.

As an example, you may have LTC benefits that will pay $5,000 a month, but that $5,000 a month might have an overall policy limit of $100,000 and, therefore, once $100,000 of benefits is paid out, you've used up that policy and there are no funds left to be paid. In that case, that $5,000 per month will pay out for twenty months, and then cease because the $100,000 benefit limit has been fully paid. When purchasing the long-term care insurance, you have to be very cognizant of both of those things. The monthly benefit and the overall policy limit are important factors and they directly affect the cost of the policy. In 2018, the average cost of long-term care is over six figures, and LTC policies have to be geared toward these costs.

The other type of insurance that can be utilized for long-term care includes what's called a "chronic illness rider." Life insurance policies, as in a regular life insurance policy that you take out (in this case, not typically including term insurance, but for whole life insurance), can include different amendments or additions to coverage called riders. These riders have varying benefits. Some have to do with payment of the premium, for example the premium being paid for you if you get sick or become disabled.

The type of rider used for long-term care planning is called a chronic illness rider, and what this rider does is it provides for payments from the policy in the event that you have a chronic illness and are in need of long-term care. If you are suffering from a chronic illness, such as dementia, and you're in need of long-term care, regardless of whether that long-term care is to take place in the home or in an institution, these long-term care riders can pay for some of those services. They do this by essentially advancing some of the life insurance death benefit to be used during your lifetime to pay for the long-term care services. The benefits paid out are later subtracted from any death benefit that is paid, but the rider takes care of the more immediate need, rather than the person having to self-pay. In my opinion, I like the chronic illness rider as a LTC planning tool much better than the old-fashioned LTC insurance and I really think that the long-term care rider is the way of the future when it comes to these policies. The old LTC insurance policies are very expensive, and they can only be used for long-term care, nothing else. There's no other benefit, so if you never go to long-term care, you never get any benefit back and all the money that you paid in was basically for nothing.

When you utilize a chronic illness rider, it's attached to a whole life policy and that whole life policy has all the same benefits that any whole life policy does. You can borrow from it. You also receive a death benefit, but it's got a chronic illness rider attached that you can utilize to pay for long-term care, if you need it. But if you end up never needing long-term care, you've still got the benefit of the cash value of the life insurance policy that you can borrow against during your lifetime, or provide a death benefit to your loved ones in the event that you pass away.

Either way, the money that you've paid in accrues a tangible benefit that gets paid out either by way of cash value of the policy or a death benefit of the policy even if you don't end up needing long-term care. It's better than LTC insurance because if you don't need long-term care, you still obtain a benefit, versus LTC insurance that only kicks in if you need long-term care, which not everyone does.

The third way to pay for long-term care is to position yourself and your assets to qualify for a Medicaid program in your state. In Massachusetts, Medicaid is run by MassHealth. For the duration of this book, we utilize the terms Medicaid and MassHealth interchangeably, but understand that Medicaid is a federal program and each state has its own way of running it and interpreting it. In Massachusetts, you can obtain MassHealth benefits for long-term care in a nursing home facility. Right now, MassHealth does not cover assisted living. They do cover nursing home facilities and in some cases, they do cover in-home care through what's called a home and community-based service waiver. With those waivers, in certain situations if you qualify, MassHealth will cover some in-home care services. But the primary use is to cover long-term care services in a nursing home. The only way to obtain that type of coverage is to qualify for MassHealth, and MassHealth has different types of qualifications, including asset and income limits. In 2018, the individual asset limit is $2,000 (BUT, through proper use of trusts, there are ways to exclude assets from this limit).

That means if you have more than $2,000 in assets, you cannot qualify for MassHealth. There are certain assets that MassHealth will accept as being uncountable and those often include the home that you live in. While they won't count the home against you when doing their asset calculation, there are ways through what's called estate asset recovery that they can attempt to put liens against the home. It's still better to make all possible moves and steps to protect your assets, and protect your home in such a way that they would be excludable from MassHealth calculations and exempt from any liens. Otherwise, if you have over $2,000 in assets, you don't qualify and you have to use your own money until you're down to that $2,000 threshold. Then you can obtain MassHealth benefits. The rules are different for a married couple, and a healthy spouse that stays in the home can have up to $123,600 in assets in 2018. While that sounds like a lot, the number drops right back down to $2,000 if that spouse later ends up needing nursing home care too. So the community spouse ends up having to spend all of that money on their own nursing home care. That's why protecting money in a proper trust can be so valuable. We can provide an evaluation to tell you your likelihood of qualifying.

People ask about gifting their assets away. Can they give their assets away to family members to get themselves down below the $2,000 limit? Not without penalty, if you intend to apply for benefits within five years of those gifts. Many clients get confused with tax rules, which allow for gifts of $15,000 or less to any beneficiary (2018 numbers) without payment of gift tax. The MassHealth penalty period is entirely different from the gift tax.

There are different rules and exceptions that can be applied, but the bottom line is that MassHealth can assert a penalty period for any assets that you gave away for less than fair market value, if given within five years of applying for benefits. They have a calculation where a certain amount of dollars that you give away equates to a certain number of days in penalty period. They look at how much you gave away in gifts, they use that to calculate the penalty period (for 2018, the figure one penalty day for every $354 given away), and they will not provide you benefits until that penalty period has passed. Further, the penalty period doesn't even start until the MassHealth applicant enters the nursing home and is otherwise eligible for benefits. That term "otherwise eligible" means that all other qualifications must be met first, before the penalty period even starts. When making their examination of gifts and other such transfers, MassHealth uses what's commonly referred to as the "five-year lookback." In other words, they look back five years from the date of your application to any gifts that you made, any transfer that you made for lower than fair market value, and then assess their penalty period for those transfers, based on the $354 per day calculation.

So how does MassHealth know that you've made any gifts or transfers? They do this by looking at bank statements and by having a pretty complicated application process that requests numerous documents. (Contact us or visit our website for a free list of documents you'll need to gather before applying.) You have to apply and include this documentation with your application, and the application process is grueling. We utilize a service that can help you gather documents needed for the application. MassHealth will actually review five years worth of statements, and they will question any withdrawals or expenditures in excess of $1,000. We do recommend, if it comes time to apply for MassHealth because you or a parent is going into long-term care, that you have a qualified attorney fill out that application for you. The attorney can then deal with any additional requests from MassHealth for more information or clarifications, which come very, very frequently.

That five-year lookback period is part of the reasons we so encourage pre-planning. The idea is to make your moves and allow five years to lapse prior to your having to apply for any MassHealth benefits. If those five years lapse, then MassHealth can't hold that transfer against you and count that asset. That's why planning early is so important and why it's such a key factor here. The best planning is done at least five years early, and allows for much better asset protection than when the client is at a point where they're going into a nursing home. If you wait until crisis point, your options are very limited because we can't make some of these transfers that we otherwise would if we had that five-year window to work with.

CHAPTER 4

PROTECTING THE HOME AND OTHER ASSETS WITH A MEDICAID TRUST

ONE OF THE most common questions that we get asked at the office is if there's a way to protect the home. How do I protect my house? Can I protect my home from a nursing home stay or from Medicaid so that if I have to go into a nursing home my children can still inherit my home? In my opinion, the best and most effective way to do this is by creating what's called a Medicaid irrevocable income-only trust, sometimes just referred to as a Medicaid trust. When done right, these trusts can protect the home, so long as (1) if the provisions of the trust are written correctly, the donor doesn't have a right to take out the trust property (there are emergency exceptions though) and (2 the transfer is made five years ahead of time. Under 2018 rules, if that home is deeded into the trust five years before applying for benefits, MassHealth cannot put a lien against the house, cannot seek to have the house sold, and can't make any other claim to that real estate. The home is protected.

As I have said, these rules are ever-changing. Written trust documents are being challenged by MassHealth all the time and estate planning and elder law attorneys have to be constantly updating their education and their documents to reflect any new cases or any new information, including the reasoning behind any new challenges to the trust documents. Further, no one can guarantee that these rules will always allow these transfers—the law can always change. But if done correctly, these trusts can help protect your home. This is a huge upside, with very little drawback. There is a free report that we offer on our website called "What Medicaid Does Not Want You to Know." There's a full discussion there of Medicaid trusts, how they work, their benefits, and their drawbacks, though we will get into the major details here as well. It is crucial if you have a Medicaid trust drafted that you have it drafted by a qualified and experienced elder law attorney. If done wrong, it can be all for nothing. If there is any way the language allows for challenges or potential holes that MassHealth can exploit, they will definitely do so.

CHAPTER 5

MEDICAID TRUST QUESTIONS AND ANSWERS

One of the best ways to give the details about Medicaid trusts is to answer the most Frequently Asked Questions we receive about those trusts. This next section will be in the form of a Q&A.

WHY USE ONE OF THESE TRUSTS?

Property put into a properly-drafted trust can be excluded from Medicaid's list of countable assets. If done right, and done early enough (remember the five-year lookback), Medicaid has no claim to the property, whether real estate or cash. When done the right way, it is the single most effective way to protect money or real estate from Medicaid/MassHealth.

DO I LOSE CONTROL OF MY PROPERTY?

No. You name a trustee to be the signatory of the trust. You reserve the right to control who the trustee is, and to change trustees at any time. If the trustee doesn't do what you want, you remove the trustee and put someone else in place. By controlling the trustee, you control the trust.

Can the trustee kick me out of my house?

No!! If the trust is holding real estate, we reserve to you the right to live there for your lifetime. This is called a "life estate" in legal terms. With a life estate, no one can kick you out—ever. And again, you control who the trustee is, so the trustee cannot sell the house without your consent.

Can Medicaid take my house?

Medicaid does not "take" the house. They will never force a spouse to move out, and they won't force a sale so long as you indicate on your application that the nursing home spouse intends to return home. BUT, they can certainly apply a lien against the house for all of the care that they pay for, and they can seek recovery of their payments from that lien and in certain circumstances also from the nursing home resident's estate after passing.

Does the Medicaid five-year lookback still apply?

Yes. That's why the rule is "the sooner, the better" when it comes to putting property into the trust. A transfer to the trust is a "gift" to the trust. Medicaid can look at any gifts you've made in the five years prior to applying for benefits. The trust needs to own the property for five years in order to get past the lookback period. It is therefore of primary importance that the property be transferred as soon as possible, to let the five-year clock start to run.

Is there a way to get my money back out of the trust?

When you put cash assets into the trust, it's best to put in money that you don't plan to take back out. In other words, for cash assets, this should be money you want to leave to your beneficiaries, rather than being paid to a nursing home or paid back to Medicaid as reimbursement for benefits conferred. You are, however, entitled to all of the income earned by the trust funds (such as bank interest or stock dividends), and can take that income at any time. There is still an emergency measure to get the money out and back to you, but it's a last resort.

CAN I DOWNSIZE OR SELL MY HOUSE?

Of course!! You have the same control over the house that you always did. You still handle the utilities the same way, taxes the same way, and insurance the same way (there are some differences with rental property). Further, with a life estate, you won't lose any real estate abatements, such as a veteran's abatement. If you are buying a new home, you don't even have to start the five-year clock over again, as long as you sell the existing home through the trust, and purchase the new home through the trust, The clock does not re-start, and the transfer date into the trust doesn't change from when you first transferred the original house by deed.

WHAT ARE THE CHANGES AS FAR AS TAXES AND CAPITAL GAINS?

There is no significant change to your beneficiaries' tax situation upon inheritance of the property from the trust. It doesn't matter what you paid for the property. The beneficiary that receives the property from your trust gets the same step-up in basis as if they inherited it from your Will. That means the fair market value on the date of your passing is the beneficiary's tax basis, or "purchase price" of the property. The capital gain on the eventual sale of the property is only the amount that is in excess of the date of death value. There is no negative tax consequence to your beneficiaries.

Why does Medicaid allow this?

For right now, it's because the law says they have no choice. The transfer to the trust is just enough of a "hands-off" situation that they don't consider you to be the "owner" of the property. By inserting the trustee, you have theoretically relinquished control, when in reality, you retain control over who the trustee is at all times.

Are these trusts expensive?

To be done correctly, these trusts require very technical expertise. Therefore, they cost more than a standard revocable trust or real estate trust. When it comes to cost, you should consider the price as an investment into keeping your home or property, when compared to paying over your hard-earned money to nursing home care.

Will this type of planning always be allowed?

The truth is that we don't know. Medicaid rules and regulations are subject to change by Congress. There can always be changes to the rules as far as the lookback period, allowance of trusts, and the like. The best planners recognize the ever-changing landscape and attend multiple continuing education classes every year. The bottom line is that if we handle your planning, and then there's a law change, you are going to hear from our office about it, and any recommended changes to your estate plan.

Is the process complicated?

The process has several moving parts (trust, deed, and trustee certificates) and can seem complicated at first viewing. When we prepare these trusts, we take special care with our clients and handle everything from drafting to implementation, with continuing guidance provided. From the client's initial telephone consult, through our streamlined online intake process, to drafting of documents, we make the process stress-free. We prepare all of the drafts, provide them to you for review, and set up a signing appointment. Painless.

WHAT ARE THE STEPS TO PUTTING ONE OF THESE TRUSTS IN PLACE?

We start with a telephone consult and then provide you with all of our recommendations and pricing. All pricing is provided at flat rates, with no guesswork and no surprises. There are no charges for phone calls or emails—ever! We prepare the trust and related documents, then, if there is real estate involved, we prepare the deed and record it for you at the Registry of Deeds. After signing, you receive a personalized binder containing all documents.

CHAPTER 6

A NOTE ABOUT MEDICAID TRUSTS FOR CASH ASSETS

As we now know from our previous chapters, the Medicaid trust might be the most effective tool for protecting the home, but the Medicaid trust can protect more than just the home. The Medicaid trust can also hold cash assets. The cash assets go into the trust and as long as they're in the trust for that five years, those assets can't be touched by MassHealth. Again, that is under current 2018 rules. The grantor, or the creator of the trust, has the right to the income generated by that cash at all times. If we open an account at a brokerage firm or with a bank, and the cash put into the trust earns interest, or dividends, or otherwise increases in value, the grantor of the trust is entitled to that income at all times. In the same manner, the trust can own rental property and that rental income is still payable to the donor at all times. However, it's a balancing act because the donor does not have the same access to the principal, which is the term for the original amount put into the trust.

There can be emergency measures where the cash assets put into the trust can be removed by the beneficiaries and gifted by the beneficiaries back to the donor, but those are emergency measures. The only cash that should go into this trust is cash that the donor is not expecting to take back out, other than the income that's earned on it. But with the use of a Medicaid trust and a carefully written estate plan, including the documents previously discussed, an individual can adequately position themselves and their assets to qualify for MassHealth benefits, yet still retain their home and other assets to pass on to their children or other beneficiaries. There are drawbacks. For example, the donor, or the creator of the trust, cannot be the trustee of the trust. The donor has to name someone else to be the trustee. That brings about the worry where a client can be afraid of losing control of their property because they're not the trustee of the property.

What the donor does retain is the right to change and replace the trustee at any time, for any reason. Because the donor controls who the trustee is, they can maintain control over the trust. If the trustee is refusing to do what the donor wants, the donor can simply replace the trustee. That's the way the donor maintains control.

CHAPTER 7

CRISIS PLANNING

THE BIGGEST ISSUE when it comes to crisis planning is the five-year lookback. With pre-planning, we take steps with the hope that we've got five years before benefits are needed. With crisis planning, almost everything we would normally do is out the window, because of the penalty period that would be assessed. We therefore have to take that penalty period into consideration with every planning technique. Crisis planning often happens when a client comes in and tells us that their mom or dad is at a point where they need to go into long-term care in a nursing home, and that they're going into that long-term care right away. If they have assets in the bank in their names, MassHealth is going to deny them benefits because they're over the $2,000 cap. That means, without crisis planning, they will have to self-pay until their assets are down under the $2,000 limit.

What will likely happen without an elder law attorney getting involved is the child will admit their parent to the nursing home, and use all the parent's money to pay for care. This could amount to $10,000, $12,000, or $15,000 a month and more. Eventually, all of the money is used up. When it's gone, they'll apply for MassHealth again and then obtain benefits that way, but all the money that the parent saved their whole life is gone. What an elder law attorney can do, even at the crisis point, is use crisis planning to help preserve some of those assets. A transfer, or a gift of those assets to somebody else, is going to bring about the penalty period because a transfer right before applying for benefits is going to be subject to the five-year lookback, the dollars are going to equate to a number of days, and a penalty period is going to be assessed before MassHealth will pay. Elder law attorneys are aware of other options that can help preserve some of these assets, even with a penalty period being assessed.

One such option is for the parent to purchase what's called a Medicaid-approved annuity. That's where a certain amount of assets can be invested into an annuity, and the annuity is paying funds back to the individual via monthly payments. What essentially happens is you've taken an asset and converted it from an asset into an income stream. MassHealth will still look at that income stream, but the applicant can drop below the asset limit by purchasing the annuity. They're still going to attribute that income to the individual and when MassHealth looks at how much they're willing to pay each month toward the nursing home cost, they also establish what's called a patient paid amount or a PPA, which acts like a monthly deductible that the applicant has to pay toward their care. They take into consideration the applicant's income, and while they allow the individual to keep a very small dollar amount, the rest of their income has to be paid to the nursing home facility. Then MassHealth steps in and pays the rest.

While they will look at the asset that you converted into an annuity and thus converted it from an asset to income, they'll look at the income and they make you pay that monthly income over to the nursing home. But it can allow you to qualify for MassHealth right away, with no penalty periods. The reason why that's beneficial is because MassHealth pays nursing homes at their own MassHealth rate, as opposed to the private pay rate, which is much higher. Think of it like when you go to the doctor's office and the doctor gives you a bill for $300, but your health insurance only pays them $100. MassHealth paying nursing homes is similar. MassHealth has a set rate they will pay to nursing homes and that's it. The private pay amount, if you're private paying, might be $15,000 a month or more, but the MassHealth rate is much, much lower. If you're going to use your own money to self-pay, you're paying at $15,000 a month. But if you take the money, convert it to an annuity, and get on MassHealth right away, now you're only paying at the MassHealth rate, which is much lower. And the money that went into the annuity is going to last much longer. If the applicant passes away later, the money left in the annuity has to be used to repay MassHealth for the benefits conferred, but anything left over after that goes to the applicant's beneficiaries. While this isn't a perfect solution, it provides an opportunity, even if it's just a chance, for some of the funds to get to the beneficiaries versus a self-pay scenario. But again, when it comes to crisis planning, sometimes some solution is better than no solution.

Another potential solution when it comes to crisis planning is to look at the assets and determine by looking at the amount of assets what type of penalty period would be applied if they gave half the assets away to one of their beneficiaries. Half of the assets can be given to a family member with the intent that the family member is going to hold those assets. The individual is going to be penalized for that transfer, using the $354 per day calculation. The amount of money that was given away equates to a number of days during which MassHealth won't pay. The individual has to self-pay during that penalty period, which is why they're giving away half the assets, instead of all.

We look at the assets overall. You've transferred half to a family member to hold, then you take the other half and you use that to buy one of these Medicaid annuities. You've converted the second half of the assets from an asset into income. You've then got no assets left. Half were given to a family member beneficiary, and half were used to purchase the annuity. You can now qualify for MassHealth, after the penalty period runs. Once again, they're still going to look at the annuity income. They're going to make you pay that income over to the nursing home as part of your patient paid amount. You design the annuity so that it coincides with the penalty period. That way, by the time the penalty period is up, the annuity payments are ending. There are no more annuity payments, so you've essentially taken half your money and used it as income to pay into the nursing home, but the other half that was transferred was protected by giving it to the family member. In theory, that family member is supposed to consider that a gift, but there's no rule that says that family member can't turn around and gift some of that back to you, use it on your behalf, and have it be left to them as inheritance when you pass. There's an alternate scenario where a promissory note is used instead of an annuity, but the concepts are the same.

You have to be very careful when doing that though, to make sure you don't violate any of Medicaid's rules. It's not something to take lightly or attempt to do on your own. A qualified elder law attorney needs to be involved.

CONCLUSION

ESTATE PLANNING AND elder law are exciting fields of law, and the best lawyers have great satisfaction in helping clients in these areas. They are ever-changing fields of law. They require constant education, constant thought, and constant creativity. The estate planning and elder law attorney has to be creative in order to come up with solutions to these various types of problems. It's very important that the attorney that you choose is experienced in this area, has specialized knowledge in this area, and is always striving to be educated in this area. You want an attorney that looks at each case individually and crafts a plan designed to your specific needs. The field of law is one where a little bit of planning ahead of time goes a long way. Doing your planning ahead, even when it causes you to have to spend money on attorney's fees to prepare certain documents, is well worth the price tag. The savings down the road can be just out of this world.

You can spend a few thousand dollars now to do some planning and save you tens or hundreds of thousands of dollars later. Do it right, and you can protect your home (which is most people's biggest asset) in a way that your home can be passed on to your beneficiaries. As we've seen, without planning, the home could be liened or lost in asset recovery to payments for nursing home care.

One of the biggest joys that I have in practicing in the estate planning and elder law fields is to take a client who maybe has a home, or maybe has some money and was of the mindset that they were going to spend all their money and potentially lose their home in paying for their care, and being able to tell that client, "Look, if we spend a few bucks now and draft some documents in a careful way, we're going to save you tens of thousands, even hundreds of thousands of dollars, that you are then going to be able to pass on to your children and your grandchildren."

When I've got a client that has worked his or her entire life to pay off their home and accrue some savings and comes to me with the fear that they're going to lose all of it and have nothing left for their kids, but I can turn around and tell them that we can protect their money, and protect it for their children, their grandchildren, and their beneficiaries by doing some planning now, I take great joy in that. This field of law is very rewarding because I get to help people solve their problems. No two cases are alike, and no two situations are exactly the same, so there's room for creativity in the planning and the types of plans to recommend for each client.

If I'm able to help a client that is going to need nursing home care, or I'm able to help children plan for Mom and Dad's care, that's something that is very fulfilling, more so than any other areas I practice. When I can help a client that has worked their whole life, or is maybe a veteran as well, and I can do something to help them protect their money, or protect what they've spent a lifetime accruing, that's life-changing for people. It is a huge burden lifted off of them to find that they're still going to be able to leave something behind for their beneficiaries and not run out of money or give all of it away to nursing home care. It takes a heavy load off of them and at the same time, makes me love going into work every day.

WA

Made in the USA
Monee, IL
23 January 2026

42218451R00059